Cambridge Elements ≡

Elements in Business Strategy
edited by
J.-C. Spender
Kozminski University

STRATEGY CONSULTING

Jeroen Kraaijenbrink
University of Amsterdam

CAMBRIDGE
UNIVERSITY PRESS

CAMBRIDGE
UNIVERSITY PRESS

University Printing House, Cambridge CB2 8BS, United Kingdom

One Liberty Plaza, 20th Floor, New York, NY 10006, USA

477 Williamstown Road, Port Melbourne, VIC 3207, Australia

314–321, 3rd Floor, Plot 3, Splendor Forum, Jasola District Centre, New Delhi – 110025, India

79 Anson Road, #06–04/06, Singapore 079906

Cambridge University Press is part of the University of Cambridge.

It furthers the University's mission by disseminating knowledge in the pursuit of education, learning, and research at the highest international levels of excellence.

www.cambridge.org
Information on this title: www.cambridge.org/9781108811958
DOI: 10.1017/9781108868365

First published 2020

A catalogue record for this publication is available from the British Library.

ISBN 978-1-108-81195-8 Paperback
ISSN 2515-0693 (online)
ISSN 2515-0685 (print)

Cambridge University Press has no responsibility for the persistence or accuracy of URLs for external or third-party internet websites referred to in this publication and does not guarantee that any content on such websites is, or will remain, accurate or appropriate.

Strategy Consulting

Elements in Business Strategy

DOI: 10.1017/9781108868365
First published online: August 2020

Jeroen Kraaijenbrink
University of Amsterdam
Author for correspondence: Jeroen Kraaijenbrink, jk@kraaijenbrink.com

Abstract: Strategy consulting is one of the most highly respected and at the same time deeply detested jobs on this planet. Despite all the attention and controversy, there is surprisingly little written about it specifically. To address this void, this Element provides a comprehensive overview of this fascinating and emerging profession. Relying on existing research and the author's practical experience, it describes what strategy consulting is, where it comes from, how to effectively practice it and where to take it into the future. Taking the position of the individual strategy consultant, this Element offers an insightful perspective that is useful for scholars, students, consultants and clients of strategy consulting. In doing so, it moves away from the dominant corporate practice of analytical strategy consulting. Instead, it offers an idealized whole-brain and whole-person view on what strategy consulting could and should be like in order to fully live up to its promise as a profession contributing to society.

Keywords: strategy consulting, whole-person consulting, strategy making, consulting roles, future of consulting

ISBNs: 9781108811958 (PB), 9781108868365 (OC)
ISSNs: 2515-0693 (online), 2515-0685 (print)

Contents

Any chief executive who hires a consultant to give them strategy should be fired.
Henry Mintzberg[1]

1 Introduction

A strategy consultant myself, I am not aware of any other job with which people have such a love–hate relationship. On the one hand, it triggers awe and envy. Although perhaps not as much as it used to be, a well-paid career as a strategy consultant is still high on the wish list of many MBA students. And within the whole market of consulting jobs, strategy consultants are on top of the hierarchy – or at least they like to think so themselves. On the other hand, strategy consultants and consultancy firms are heavily criticized both by scholars writing about them and executives having worked with them. If you ask them, they are quite critical about strategy consultants' added value, ethics and way of working. Illustrative for this critical perspective are books about consulting, baring titles such as *Dangerous Company* (O'Shea & Madigan, 1998), *Consulting Demons* (Pinault, 2009) and *The Witch Doctors* (Micklethwait & Wooldridge, 1996).

Of all consulting firms, both the awe and the criticism apply strongest to McKinsey & Company – or McKinsey in short. And along with it, they also apply to other major consulting firms such as the Boston Consulting Group, Bain & Company, A. T. Kearney and Booz Allen Hamilton. It seems you either love them or you hate them – or both at the same time. This paradoxical attitude towards strategy consulting is insightful. The very fact that companies hire strategy consultants and pay significant amounts of money for their services shows that they serve an important purpose that is valued by their customers. At the same time, though, the sheer volume and severity of criticisms are strong indicators that something is not entirely right about strategy consulting as it is practised today.

The purpose of this Element is therefore to explore what strategy consulting is, what it should lead to and how it can be practised effectively. I focus specifically on strategy consulting because, surprisingly, despite its impact and controversy, there is not so much written about it. There are numerous works on management consulting in general (Baaij, 2013; Kipping & Clark, 2012; Newton, 2010) and even more so on strategy and on consulting at large. But on the specifics of strategy consulting, with the exception of a few (Armbrüster & Kipping, 2002; Blom & Lundgren, 2013; Delany, 1995; Payne & Lumsden, 1987; Van den Bosch, Baaij, & Volberda, 2005), there is a clear void. With this Element I intend to help fill this void from a dual perspective. As

---

[1] Interview by Duff McDonald on 7 April 2010, as quoted in McDonald (2013).

a scholar, I aim to give a balanced overview of the research others have done on strategy consulting and the experiences they have described. I will add to that my own views and experience as strategy consultant. By combining these 'outsider' and 'insider' views, this Element intends to offer a fresh perspective on the specifics of strategy consulting that goes beyond the status quo.

1.1 Related Work

Even though not much has been written specifically on strategy consulting, there is an extensive body of literature on management consulting more broadly. Since strategy consulting is a part of that, much of that literature is relevant for strategy consulting as well. Therefore, as a starting point of this Element, I will briefly outline the five main types of publication available. This helps demarcate what this Element is about and is not about, and it serves as a point of reference for further reading.

The first type of publication is comprehensive work that provides an almost encyclopaedic overview of what management consulting entails, where it comes from and how it works. I will single out three of them. The first is the over 800-page reference work *Management Consulting: A Guide to the Profession*, edited by Milan Kubr (2002). Targeted primarily at (prospective) consultants, it contains contributions by numerous authors, giving an in-depth practical understanding of management and strategy consulting. A second reference work is *The Oxford Handbook of Management Consulting*, edited by Matthias Kipping and Timothy Clark (2012). It targets academics and as such offers a more theoretical understanding of the field and outlines avenues for further research. Third, I will mention McKenna's (2006) *The World's Newest Profession: Management Consulting in the Twentieth Century*. It is a single-authored and widely praised historical analysis of management consulting and offers a fascinating and deep understanding of management consulting as an emerging profession. For getting a thorough understanding of management consulting and strategy consulting as they have been practised and studied over the past century, all three works are recommended.

Also comprehensive, but more instrumental are the various management consulting textbooks that have been written. Strategy and management consulting are high on the wish list of many MBA students. Numerous textbooks facilitate courses on this topic. Three examples are Marc Baaij's *An Introduction to Management Consultancy* (Baaij, 2013), Philip Wickham and Jeremy Wilcock's *Management Consulting: Delivering an Effective Project* (Wickham & Wilcock, 2016) and Joe O'Mahoney and Calvert Markham's *Management Consultancy* (O'Mahoney & Markham, 2013). These are comprehensive textbooks giving a representative view of what management consulting in large consulting corporations looks like. They typically combine an overview of the consulting history and industry with more instrumental advice as to how to consult in practice.

On the practical side, there are also books directly targeted at the aspiring or practising consultant. With their first editions printed in 1981 and 1992 and many copies sold, Peter Block's *Flawless Consulting: A Guide to Getting Your Expertise Used* (Block, 2000) and Alan Weiss' *Million Dollar Consulting: The Professional Guide to Growing a Practice* (Weiss, 1992) are amongst the most influential of such books. They offer extensive prescriptions on how to be an effective consultant. Another example is Richard Newton's *The Management Consultant: Mastering the Art of Consultancy*. Although it covers similar contents, the fact that it is written from a more personal perspective makes it a useful additional read. A fourth book in this category is *The Trusted Advisor* by David Maister, Charles Green and Robert Galford (Maister, Green, & Galford, 2000). Like the previous three, this book is an instrumental work, explaining to the reader how to become a trusted advisor. It is particularly worth reading because of its focus on the concept of the trusted advisor, rather than management consultancy. I will return to what this means and why it is relevant later in this Element.

Fourth, also instrumental, are works describing the approach of a specific consulting firm. Unlike the previous three categories, these books zoom in on one consulting company and explain in detail how management consulting works at that particular company. The clear majority of these books is about McKinsey. Examples include *The McKinsey Way* by Ethan Rasiel (1999), *The McKinsey Mind* by Ethan Rasiel and Paul Friga (2001), *The Pyramid Principle* by Barbara Minto (2009) and *The Firm: The Inside Story of McKinsey: The World's Most Controversial Management Consultancy* by Duff McDonald (2013). The first three are written by (ex-)'McKinsey-ites' actively promoting and distributing the way McKinsey works. As such, they offer an insider's view on what it means to work for the world's most dominant consulting firm. They are revealing, not merely because of their contents but also because of the style in which they are written. McDonald's work is different. It offers a deep peek into the inner workings of McKinsey over time. It is a more neutral and comprehensive analysis of McKinsey that reveals both its strengths and its weaknesses.

Finally, there are the critiques already referred to earlier: James O'Shea's and Charles Madigan's *Dangerous Company: Management Consultants and the Businesses They Save and Ruin* (O'Shea & Madigan, 1998), Lewis Pinault's *Consulting Demons: Inside the Unscrupulous World of Global*

Corporate Consulting (Pinault, 2009) and John Micklethwait and Adrian Wooldbridge's *The Witch Doctors: What the Management Gurus Are Saying, Why It Matters and How to Make Sense of It* (Micklethwait & Woodridge, 1996). These are polemical works criticizing management consulting from various perspectives. Less polemical but critical too is *Critical Consulting: New Perspectives on the Management Advice Industry*, edited by Timothy Clark and Robin Fincham (2002). It primarily emphasizes the rhetorical character of much management consulting. Also insightful is Richard Rumelt's *Good Strategy/Bad Strategy: The Difference and Why It Matters* (Rumelt, 2011). It is a criticism not of strategy consulting per se but of strategy in general. However, given that strategy consultants are amongst the most important causes of 'bad strategy', it does provide useful insights into their work. A sixth work in this category is Ewald Weiden's *Folienkrieg und Bullshitbingo: Handbuch für Unternehmensberater, Opfer und Angehörige* (Slide War and Bullshit Bingo: Manual for Management Consultants, Victims and Relatives) (Weiden, 2014). It is more a parody approaching management consulting with a strike of humour. Its main added value is that it helps take consulting and consultants not too seriously. Together, the critical approach in these works makes them worth reading because it helps understand some of the weaknesses and downsides of management and strategy consulting as it has been practised so far. By highlighting these, they show where improvement is needed to take strategy consulting to the next level.

Altogether these books offer a thorough and balanced view of what management consulting looks like so far, how it has evolved to get there and what the upsides and downsides are. And even though they concern management consulting at large, much of what they say applies directly to strategy consulting. This Element will therefore not repeat for strategy consulting what these works have already said. This means this Element will not attempt to provide a comprehensive overview of strategy consulting, nor does it explain how the big consulting firms do strategy consulting. And, even though it will contain critical notes, it is not a polemical attack on strategy consulting.

The main aim of this Element is to look forward and sketch what strategy consulting could, and perhaps even should, look like in the future in order to fully live up to its promise as a profession contributing to society. Therefore, what this Element contains is more an idealized future perspective than an accurate or representative account of strategy consulting today. As it unfolds in the next sections, this leads to a whole-brain, whole-person view on strategy consulting that moves beyond the dominant practice of analytical strategy consulting.

1.2 Defining Strategy Consulting

For discussing strategy consulting, it is useful to first define what it means. The goal of this is not to come up with a final or an all-encompassing definition. The goal is to provide the foundation on which the view on strategy consulting outlined in this Element is based. Since both parts of the term 'strategy consulting' are up for discussion, I will first define them separately.

1.2.1 Strategy

There are almost as many definitions of strategy as there are authors writing about them. This means that any attempt to define strategy will introduce debates and disagreements. Nevertheless, to define strategy consulting, it is essential to define what we mean by strategy. This is not only important to demarcate the differences between strategy and other types of consulting. It also affects what strategy consulting could and should be.

As explained in two earlier books – *The Strategy Handbook*, parts 1 and 2 (Kraaijenbrink, 2015, 2018) – I define strategy as an organization's unique way of sustainable value creation. It means that an organization's strategy expresses which value it creates for whom, and how it does this in a way that differentiates it from its main competitors and so that it can sustain this difference for a longer period of time.

This definition is neither unique nor original. It relies on various previous definitions, most notably on the foundational work of Michael Porter (1980, 1991) and Henry Mintzberg (1987, Mintzberg & Waters, 1985). But its emphasis on value creation, uniqueness, sustainability and the 'way' organizations achieve these, points to four important aspects:

- The focus is on value creation, not on creating competitive advantage as in many other definitions. Of course, having a competitive advantage as an organization is helpful. But it is only a means towards unique and sustainable value creation, not a goal in itself. The reason of existence of any organization is the value it creates for its customers. Therefore, value creation is centre stage in strategy.
- The emphasis on uniqueness means that strategy aims at standing out compared to the competition. It implies that a strategy reflects how an organization aims to be different from its most relevant competitors. Ideally, this difference reflects both the organization's unique strengths and the specific needs of the customers it targets.
- The focus on sustainability means that strategy has a long-term orientation. A strategy is sustainable when it provides the organization with sufficient

returns, when it is not based on resources that are soon to be depleted, when it considers key stakeholders' interests and when it is hard to imitate or circumvent by others. If any of these four requirements is not met, a strategy is not really sustainable.

- Strategy concerns the way organizations try to realize the previous three aspects. It is not a plan, a document, a set of goals, aspirations or wishes. It is a way, a series of steps or actions that enables an organization to create value in a unique and sustainable way. And given that both the organization and its environment change continuously, this way is never fixed. This means that strategy is a continuous process that never stops or starts.

This brief definition of what strategy means has important implications for strategy consulting. As we will see in Sections 5 and 6, the continuous, action-oriented nature of strategy that results from it has significant implications for what strategy consultants can and cannot do and what the strategy consulting process looks like. Furthermore, as argued in Section 4, its focus on sustainable value creation also has significant implications for the purpose and outcomes strategy consulting should be looking for.

1.2.2 Consulting

Like with strategy, numerous definitions of consulting exist. Examples include 'Any form of providing help on the content, process, or structure of a task or series of tasks, where the consultant is not actually responsible for doing the task itself but is helping those who are' (Steele, 1975, p. 3), 'you are consulting any time you are trying to change or improve a situation but have no direct control over the implementation' (Block, 2000, p. xxi) and 'Management consultancy is thus a form of situation-specific assistance provided by an independent, external and professional intervention-expert who enables the management of a client's organization to take action in an over complex management situation' (Hagenmeyer, 2007, p. 110). While they differ, together these definitions highlight a number of characteristics defining consulting:

- **External:** a consultant is an outsider that supports an organization or organizational unit but is not a part of it. This also applies to consultants within organizations: they are outsiders to the units they consult.
- **Independence:** while never 100 percent independent – as their income depends on the consulting assignment – a consultant is as independent as possible. This means that they have no personal stake in the issue they consult on or the solution that is sought for.

- **Professionals:** consultants are qualified individuals who have the relevant mindset, experience, skills and expertise needed to support their clients. They have high standards and are committed to doing the best for their clients.
- **Support:** consultants help organizations solve problems, execute tasks or achieve goals that they cannot do on their own. This also means that consultants are not responsible for or in control of what they consult on.
- **Change:** a consultant initiates, designs, facilitates and/or executes change in organizations. Their task is to help an organization make those improvements that help it survive and prosper.

Along these lines, a consultant is an external and independent professional supporting organizations make changes. Consulting then is providing organizations support with making changes as an external and independent professional.

1.2.3 Strategy Consulting

Combining the two aforementioned definitions, strategy consulting is providing organizations support with making changes to achieve unique and sustainable value creation as an external and independent professional. Or simply, helping organizations achieve unique and sustainable value creation as an external and independent professional. With this simple definition as a starting point, we can now dive deeper and scrutinize in detail in this Element what strategy consulting entails and how to do it.

Before we do so, we need to make two more observations to complement this definition. First, strategy consulting is not something reserved for big corporations, neither on the client's side nor on the consultant's side. All organizations need strategy, no matter how small they are. Even independent freelancers need to have a unique and sustainable way of value creation to survive and prosper. And strategy consultancies can be large firms, small firms or independent consultants. All of them can provide their clients with support with making changes as external and independent professionals. Therefore, whatever is said about strategy consulting in this Element applies to these various types of consultancies and clients.

Second, while the definition is simple, strategy consulting is complex. As Kubr (2002) reminds us, it is both multidisciplinary (involving social, psychological, legal, technological aspects etc.) and multifunctional (concerning marketing, production, engineering, finance, HR, R&D etc.). This multi-sidedness of strategy makes strategy consulting one of the most complex types of consulting. Even though other functions such as marketing, engineering or finance have their own internal complexities, the very fact that strategy concerns their integration adds another level of complexity to strategy consulting. When we furthermore add that strategy takes place in an environment characterized by high volatility and uncertainty, it is obvious that strategy consulting is a challenging job. More importantly, and as referred to in the introductory quote, it means that strategy consultancy is about many things – but not about something as static and disengaged as providing an organization with a strategy.

1.3 Strategy Consulting as Profession

The words 'profession' and 'professional' have appeared several times in the aforementioned text. This brings us to the decades-old discussion about whether management consulting – and therefore also strategy consulting – is a profession or not. McKenna (2006) and Kubr (2002), for example, explicitly use the word profession in the title of their books and also several other aforementioned works explicitly address this question. Therefore, it needs to be addressed in this Element as well.

1.3.1 Why It Matters

The question of whether strategy consulting is a profession is part of a broader discussion on whether or not management and strategy are a profession and whether they should be (Khurana, 2007; Rousseau, 2012; Spender, 2007). The sheer attention that is given to this question by academics suggests it matters. And it does, for two reasons.

The first reason is that, through their language and behaviours, strategy consultancies tend to present themselves as professionals and their job as a profession. By doing so, they suggest that they are like, for example, healthcare providers, lawyers and accountants, following agreed-upon practices, rules and guidelines. If this is how they present themselves, it is legitimate to ask whether they rightfully do so. Because if this is not the case, this may challenge consultants' credibility and ethics.

The second reason is that, if strategy consulting is or aspires to be a profession, then the ideas of what a profession entails serve as a frame of reference to assess current strategy consulting practice. We can then assess whether strategy consulting fulfils the criteria of being a profession. And where it does not, this provides directions for where strategy consulting should go. In other words, if strategy consulting aspires to be a profession, then the criteria of professions provide a normative framework for what strategy consulting should entail.

1.3.2 What It Means

Whether strategy consulting is a profession or not depends on how we identify whether something is a profession. There are three ways to do this. The first is a trait-based approach. It means listing the traits of a profession and assess whether strategy consulting has these traits. Traits that are mentioned include (1) one or more professional associations, (2) formal training and certification, (3) a standardized and shared body of knowledge, (4) a code of ethics to which one commits, (5) professional liability for the work done, (6) self-discipline and self-regulation and (7) a focus on contributing to the greater good (Baaij, 2013; Kipping & Clark, 2012; Kubr, 2002; McKenna, 2006).

A second way to assess whether strategy consulting is a profession is to follow a developmental approach. This means looking at whether the stakeholders involved in strategy consulting are currently taking the required actions needed to turn it into a profession. This means assessing whether a deliberate, conscious and coordinated attempt is going on to translate a set of scarce cultural and technical resources into a secure and institutionalized system of social and financial rewards (Kirkpatrick, Muzio, & Ackroyd, 2012).

A third way is to not look so much at whether the field is or is developing into a profession, but to look whether strategy consultants act as professionals and follow a professional approach. This includes having appropriate competences, avoiding conflicts of interest, being impartial and objective, treating sensitive information confidentially, not accepting inappropriate payments, offering good value for money and taking into account a wider social concern and ethical principles (Kubr, 2002).

1.3.3 Whether Strategy Consulting Is a Profession

Evaluated against the seven traits of the first approach, there is a widely shared conclusion that management consulting, and thereby strategy consulting implied, is at best an emerging profession. We find this conclusion most clearly in the work of McKenna (2006), but also in other works including those of Kubr (2002), Baaij (2013), Kipping and Clark (2012) and Greiner, Motamedi, and Jamieson (2011). All of them conclude that management consulting hardly qualifies as a profession on any of the seven traits. There are, for example, professional institutions (such as the International Council of Management Consulting Institutes, ICMCI), but their membership is low and they have no authority. As mentioned on their website, for example, ICMCI represents 64,200 individual consultants. This is less than 10 percent of the total number of management consultants in the United States alone.[2] Also, there is a lot of strategy consulting training, but this is mostly given within the boundaries of a single consulting firm and focused on distinction rather than on creating a shared body of knowledge. Furthermore, there is no shared code of ethics,

---

[2] www.statista.com/statistics/419968/number-of-management-consultants-us/, numbers for 2018.

no professional liability, no self-regulation, and no clear focus on the greater good. In this light, as practised today, strategy consulting is clearly not a profession.

When following the developmental approach, the conclusion is similar. Even though strategy consulting presents itself often as a profession, there are no signs that it is developing in that direction. There are scattered initiatives, for example by the ICMCI, but there are no widely spread or coordinated attempts to realize this. And this is not surprising. As McKenna (2006) and Kirkpatrick, Muzio, and Ackroyd (2012) observe, consultancies have no interest to develop into a profession because professionalization would only constrain them. Currently they benefit from their professional image without the constraints and responsibilities that come with being an actual profession.

According to the first two approaches, we can conclude that strategy consulting is neither a profession nor developing in that direction. However, there seems to be some agreement that strategy consultants do follow a professional approach. While there always will be exceptions, the large majority of strategy consultants does work in the manner Kubr describes earlier – they have relevant competences, avoid conflicts of interest, try to be impartial and objective and so on. Together these three brief assessments lead to a straightforward conclusion: strategy consultants are professionals but they don't function as a profession nor are they developing in that direction.

1.3.4 Whether Strategy Consulting Should Be a Profession

A final important question is whether strategy consulting should be a profession. We can take two perspectives here: a societal perspective and an individual perspective. When adopting a societal perspective, the answer seems clearly confirmative. As argued and well supported with evidence and examples in the comprehensive works referred to (Kipping & Clark, 2012; Kubr, 2002; McKenna, 2006) and the critical ones (McDonald, 2013; Micklethwait & Wooldridge, 1996; O'Shea & Madigan, 1998; Pinault, 2009), consultancies have had a significant role in the failure of many of their clients and also in stimulating illegal and unethical practices – the Enron scandal and McKinsey's involvement in it being the most notable example. Therefore, from a societal perspective one could easily argue that their unconstrained power and self-interested behaviour ought to be constrained by institutionalization, formal training, certification and self-regulation.

Answering that same question from my personal perspective as a strategy consultant, though, leads to a different answer. As a consultant, I don't want to be constrained. I like the freedom I have and the fact that there are no standards dictating how I should work. Furthermore, I don't need an institution legitimizing what I do, I don't believe formal training is going to make me a better consultant and I don't think that certification or institutional membership will increase my credibility. And also I don't think that regulation or a code of ethics will make me behave more ethical or focus more on contributing to the greater good. These are things I inherently intend to do anyway. The conclusion from a personal standpoint as strategy consultant is therefore clear as well: I don't think further professionalization is needed and I would even object to it, especially if it means formalization and adherence to norms and regulations imposed by institutions.

What follows from these two opposing perspectives is that even though many of the aspired effects of professionalization are desired given the criticisms on consulting, the way forward is not necessarily a systemic attempt towards professionalization. I expect that many other consultants will object for similar reasons as I do. Furthermore, because of all the vested interests by large and powerful consulting corporations, it is very unlikely that there will be any significant progress towards more institutionalized professionalization in the foreseeable future. As a result, bottom-up, gradual change by individual consultants adjusting their approach and mindset may be the best and only way forward. It is along those lines and with this intention that this Element was written.

1.4 An Idealist Perspective on Strategy Consulting

This Element provides an idealist perspective on strategy consulting. This means that it offers a perspective on what strategy consulting could, or even should look like. Given the criticisms, it is not enough to just describe what strategy consulting is like today. Furthermore, as referred to in Section 1.1, others have already done this before. Therefore, what follows is a forward-looking perspective on strategy consulting that moves beyond the status quo and that addresses the criticism.

1.4.1 Pseudo Consulting

There are various reasons strategy consultants are hired that may be useful and legitimate, but that can be considered 'pseudo consulting' because no actual consulting takes place. These are cases where strategy consultants are primarily hired for rhetorical reasons or as scapegoat. While it applies to many consulting firms, especially McKinsey is known for being hired to legitimate and implement decisions that have already been made or to take the blame for them along the idea 'McKinsey is saying it, so it must be true'. In those cases, hiring strategy consultants is primarily a rhetorical act to enforce a previously made decision. Such type of pseudo consulting is outside the scope of this Element.

Some critical scholars go even as far as defining consultants first and foremost as fad bringers and rhetoricians. Nikolova and Devinney (2012) call this the 'critical model' of consulting, thereby referring to the view on consulting offered by, amongst others, Alvesson (2002) and Clark (1995). The key point of that model of consulting is that consultants are specialists in impression management – in giving clients the impression that they buy something valuable, often without much actual value being created. While this may be an overly critical interpretation of consulting in general, it does occur. Also this type of consulting is outside the scope of this Element.

What this Element does focus on is 'genuine' strategy consulting that is aimed at helping clients forward with their strategy. Or, along the lines of the definition given earlier, the work that is focused on helping organizations achieve unique and sustainable value creation as an external and independent professional.

1.4.2 A Whole-Person Approach to Strategy Consulting

The approach to strategy consulting outlined in this Element can be described as a 'whole-brain, whole-person' approach. The details of this approach will unfold throughout the next sections, but the overall idea can be summarized as follows. So far, strategy consulting is largely a left-brain activity. It has a strong fact-based, cognitive-analytical focus aimed at deconstructing and solving problems in a scientific or engineering fashion. However, the right part of the brain, which is associated with creativity, intuition, holistic thinking, empathy and self-awareness is largely ignored. Given that strategy consulting requires both halves and given that we are all endorsed with two brain halves, it is evident that, to be effective, a 'whole-brain' approach to strategy consulting is needed.

Even further, we need a 'whole-person' approach to strategy consulting. So far, strategy consulting is primarily a head-only activity. The image of strategy consultants that we get from descriptions so far is that of cold 'talking heads' that are supposed to switch off their emotions, provide clinical advice and are not supposed to get their hands dirty. But next to a head, people have a heart and hands too. Not using those in strategy consulting in today's challenging environment is a waste of potential. Furthermore, actually helping organizations make changes requires strategy consultants to use their full capacity as human beings – including their specific character, preferences, aspirations, viewpoints and emotions.

There is another reason why a whole-brain, whole-person approach to strategy consulting is needed: it is increasingly what the next generation of employees is looking for. As various studies reveal, people entering the labour market increasingly look for interesting jobs that give them the freedom to be themselves and that provide them with a sense of contribution[3]. People increasingly want to make a difference. In the competition for talent, a whole-brain, whole-person approach can help to ensure that becoming a strategy consultant remains an attractive career choice.

1.5 Organization of Sections

This Element is organized as follows. Section 2 offers a brief overview of the history of strategy, thereby primarily focusing on why it exists and how it came into being. Section 3 summarizes the traditional mode of consulting and the criticism it has received. Together, these two sections set the stage and provide an understanding of what strategy consulting has been like so far. The next three sections outline a view on strategy consulting that departs from this and takes strategy consulting towards the future. Section 4 discusses the purpose and outcome of strategy consulting, Section 5 the strategy consulting process and Section 6 the various roles strategy consultants play throughout this process. The Element ends in Section 7 with a conclusion and outlook.

2 The Origins of Strategy Consulting

Like any field, strategy consulting has a specific history. Describing management consulting more broadly, and thereby including strategy consulting, this history has been extensively covered in previous works (Kipping & Clark, 2012; Kubr, 2002; McDonald, 2013; McKenna, 2006). Instead of repeating their comprehensive accounts, this section follows a different approach. It starts with providing a very brief summary of the history of strategy consulting so that the basic development of the field is understood. Thereafter, Section 2.2 provides an inventory of the various explanations of why strategy consulting exists. This provides an understanding of why and how strategy consulting works the way it does. The section concludes by offering an alternative history in Section 2.3. The reason is that, if the premise on which this Element rests – that strategy consulting should be different in the future than today – is correct, alternative perspectives come in that have their own history.

---

[3] www2.deloitte.com/global/en/pages/about-deloitte/articles/millennialsurvey.html
www.accenture.com/us-en/insights/strategy/whole-brain-leadership-for-c-suites

2.1 A Very Brief History of Strategy Consulting

To understand where strategy consulting comes from, it is useful to summarize some of the key historical facts and developments as they have taken place over the past century. They are:

- **1870–1900:** industrial revolution, going hand in hand with the emergence of the first field of consulting: operations consultancy. With its roots in engineering and the influential work of Frederick W. Taylor, Harrington Emerson and Charles Eugène Bedaux, the focus was on improving efficiency.
- **1910–1930:** development of the second field of consulting: organizational consulting. Parallel to the emergence of the multidivisional corporate form and building upon ideas from engineering too, consultancies like Arthur D. Little (1909), Booz Allen & Hamilton (1914) and McKinsey & Company (1926) were founded. They focused on solving organizational issues by designing and changing organizational structures and processes.
- **1910–1950:** in parallel to organizational consulting, the field of human relations and organizational development (OD) emerged as a field of consulting. Notable contributions were Mayo's Hawthorne studies (published in 1933), John D. Rockefeller's financial support and industrial relations and Eric Trist's work at the Tavistock institute from 1945 on.
- **1950–1960:** as a result of the first mainframe computers, development of IT consultancy as new consulting discipline. Especially IBM (founded 1924) played an influential role in advancing this discipline.
- **1960–1980:** emergence of strategy consulting as separate discipline, most notably by the foundation of the Boston Consulting Group in 1963, Roland Berger in 1967 and Bain & Company in 1973, where it is useful to notice that both Roland Berger and Bill Bain were BCG alumni.

Other interesting facts are the roles of US legislators, the military and business schools (David, 2012), as well as the development of the strategy consulting sector between 1980 and today (Kipping & Clark, 2012). But it is this early history that helps understand where strategy consulting comes from. Important to notice is the field's engineering roots, evidenced by strategy consulting's direct predecessors operations and organizational consulting. Also important to notice is the role of the Boston Consulting Group. It is this consulting firm where strategy consulting started. And it is their growth-share matrix (or BCG matrix, with its cash cows, stars, question marks and dogs) that was the first main strategy consulting tool (McDonald, 2013).

2.2 Why Strategy Consulting Exists

To understand what strategy consulting is we should not only look at the historical development, but also develop a better understanding of why it exists in the first place. This reveals why strategy consulting works the way it does and why it has developed in the way it has. Across the literature, there are no less than ten alternative, partly overlapping, but nevertheless distinct and complementary explanations.

2.2.1 Economic Perspective

A widely used explanation of why strategy consultancy exists is because specializing in strategy involves economies of knowledge (Saam, 2012). Like with other specialized services, the idea is that consultants can develop and accumulate advanced specialized knowledge in strategy by working with different organizations. Since every single organization can only develop this knowledge for itself, consultants thereby have a knowledge advantage. As such, they can benefit from information asymmetries and economies of knowledge by developing advanced knowledge and reusing it at various clients.

2.2.2 Resource-Based Perspective

A closely related, but more strategic perspective is that strategy consultants can obtain and develop valuable, rare, inimitable and non-substitutable resources and capabilities that provide them with a competitive advantage that they can exploit. While most of the assumptions are similar as in the economic perspective, this resource-based view (Barney, 1991; Kraaijenbrink, Spender, & Groen, 2010) emphasizes more the value that firms can create by offering strategy consulting services rather than the efficiencies that can be achieved.

2.2.3 Institutional Perspective

Another, more historically oriented explanation can be found by looking at the conditions and institutions that played a role in shaping the strategy consulting market. As David (2012), McDonald (2013) and McKenna (2006, 2012) show, developments in legislation, business schools, the military situation and the business press created the conditions under which strategy consulting could develop and flourish. As such, strategy consulting can be seen as an expected, almost inevitable response to these conditions.

2.2.4 Organizational Perspective

Parallel to the developments in society, the emergence of strategy consulting can also be explained by looking at organizations themselves. As David (2012) points out, the development of the multi-divisional form of corporations, with its dispersed and decentralized units has made them so complex and hard to manage, that this created the opportunity for strategy consultants to step in. Related is that many organizations today have marginalized their strategy knowledge and processes to such an extent that they have difficulties managing strategy themselves, thereby opening the door for strategy consultants.

2.2.5 Isomorphism Perspective

In deciding whether or not to adopt certain practices, managers often look at other organizations. The idea is that, if others do it, it is probably useful for them to do it too. This is called isomorphism (DiMaggio & Powell, 1983), and this also plays a role in the adoption of strategy consultants. As a result of the first four perspectives, the idea has emerged that hiring consultants for strategy is the right thing to do. This applies in particular to the strategy generation phase. Because other managers are hiring strategy consultants, managers think they should hire them too. Isomorphism keeps this idea alive, even when the original reasons for hiring strategy consultants don't apply anymore.

2.2.6 Mystification Perspective

Strategy consulting, as well as other types of strategy services like strategy education and publication, benefits from actively mystifying the notion of strategy and that of consulting. As we learn in textbooks and MBA courses, strategy must by high level and abstract, because, as soon as it becomes more practical and operational, it is not a strategy anymore. The deliberate secrecy surrounding the large strategy consulting firms contributes further to this mystification. As a result of this mystification, managers may feel incapable of proper strategizing, thereby creating opportunities for strategy consultants.

2.2.7 Enlightenment Perspective

As a result of a centuries-long development that is going on since the Enlightenment in 18th Century Europe (or arguably even since Plato, 400 BC), we are conditioned to think that scientific, rational-analytic approaches are the best or even only way to solve problems. Strategy consultancies are experts at solving problems in this way. Thereby, they allude to this almost built-in idea that we have, which makes them attractive to hire. The idea is that, if problems should be addressed in a rational-analytic way, and if strategy consultants are the experts, they are the ones that should be asked to solve the problem.

2.2.8 Marketing Perspective

The success of strategy consultancy can also be understood by looking at it from a marketing and sales perspective. As various scholars have argued, strategy consultancies and in particular consulting gurus play a central role in creating and distributing management fads and fashions (Abrahamson, 1996; Clark, Bhatanacharioen, & Greatbatch, 2012; Jung & Kieser, 2012). By introducing new information, frameworks and tools and publishing about them, consultancies actively create and maintain both the demand and the supply for their services.

2.2.9 Sociological Perspective

The success of strategy consulting can also be understood from a sociological network perspective (Faust, 2012). Strategy consultancy's reputation and network position provide them with various benefits that make them attractive partners for organizations. They are often well connected and respected and use these network-based strengths to their advantage. Furthermore, by having many of their alumni working for other organizations, strategy consultancies often have strong ties with clients and prospective clients.

2.2.10 Career Perspective

A last perspective explaining why strategy consulting exists is that it is, for some, an attractive career choice. It offers a good salary and status, interesting clients and travelling destinations and working on top-level organizational issues without having the responsibility for them. As Lemann (1999) puts it, it is the 'odd upper-meritocratic combination of love of competition, herd mentality, and aversion to risk' that makes a consulting job so appealing (McKenna, 2006). This attractiveness makes that many highly qualified students apply for a job as strategy consultant.

As these ten perspectives show, the reasons why strategy consulting is what it is and has grown to such an extensive business are multifold. In isolation they all provide partial explanations, but altogether they help us understand why strategy consulting has become the influential business it is today. These perspectives also reveal how and why strategy consulting works. We see, for example, that it works through developing and exploiting specialized generic strategy knowledge across clients (#1) and developing tools and active publication to create awareness and demand for their services (#8), thereby filling a void that organizations have created themselves (#4).

2.3 An Alternative History

The above brief history and perspectives help us understand how strategy consulting as we currently know it has emerged. This is helpful. But it is not enough if we want to look forward to where strategy consulting may be or should be heading. If, as suggested in Section 1.4, this is a whole-brain, whole-person approach to strategy, then knowing the history of strategy consulting as we know it is not enough. In particular the development of HR and OD consulting become a crucial part of its history too because these complement the left-brain orientation of strategy consulting as we know it.

While its engineering roots can be seen as strategy consulting's father, responsible for its left-brain focus, HR/OD consulting can be seen as its mother – and more responsible for the right-brain part that is mostly missing so far. Section 2.1 already briefly mentioned the work of Mayo and Trist as important contributions to this field of consulting. Because it is less emphasized in accounts of strategy consulting's history, it is worthwhile giving it more attention at this place.

As the next section will show in more detail, the mode of strategy consulting that has emerged from engineering is expert consulting. Strategy consultants are supposed to come up with solid analyses, leading to well-founded answers. HR/OD consulting, on the other side, is more process and people oriented (Greiner et al., 2011). Also, whereas strategy consulting adopts primarily a problem-solving approach (focused on fixing what is wrong), HR/OD consulting focuses much more on building upon an organization's strengths and aspirations.

Foundational contributions to the development of this line of thinking come from Mary Parker Follett in the 1920s (Follett, 1924; Follett, Fox, & Urwick, 1973). Unlike her well-known contemporary Frederick W. Tayler and his 'Scientific Management' (Taylor, 1911), Follett outlines a view on management and organizations that is people and development-oriented. Her work has been the source of many HR/OD-related ideas such as consent-based decision-making, transformational leadership, reciprocal relationships, integrative and holistic thinking, diversity and the importance of informal processes. Ever since, many others have built on Follet's ideas, including Kurt Lewin (1948), Douglas McGregor (1960), Abraham Maslow (1970) and Chris Argyris (Chris Argyris, Putnam, & McLain Smith, 1985; Argyris & Schön, 1978).

While all of them have significantly influenced HR/OD consulting, there is one approach worthwhile mentioning specifically because it most explicitly focuses on consulting and is both deviating from and complementary to the traditional strategy consulting approach: appreciative inquiry (Cooperrider & Srivastva, 1987; Whitney & Cooperrider, 2005). The core idea of appreciative inquiry is to start with what already works in an organization and build further upon that. It is 'the cooperative, coevolutionary search for the best in people, their organizations, and the relevant world around them. It involves systematic discovery of what gives life to an organization or a community when it is most effective, and most capable in economic, ecological, and human terms' (Whitney & Cooperrider, 2005, p. 8). While its principles and approach need not necessarily be fully adopted, the next sections will show how embracing some of the core principles of appreciative inquiry helps developing a whole-brain, whole-person approach to strategy consulting.

3 Traditional Strategy Consulting and Its Limitations

As a result of the specific history outlined in the previous section, a dominant approach to strategy consulting has emerged over the past decades. I will refer to this as the traditional approach to strategy consulting. Because it is the dominant approach and the source of much criticism, it is important to understand this approach when we want to move forward. To stay brief and focused, the description is limited to McKinsey's approach. While it will not be fully representative, it is the best documented and most influential approach applied and taught across this globe. Furthermore, because various other consulting firms have their origins inside McKinsey too, its approach is in the DNA of the sector.

3.1 The Traditional Strategy Consulting Approach

Overall, the traditional approach to strategy consulting can be best summarized as an expert approach. It is described in general in textbooks (Baaij, 2013; Newton, 2010) and more specifically in accounts of McKinsey's way of working (McDonald, 2013; Minto, 2009; Rasiel, 1999; Rasiel & Friga, 2001). It has the following twelve characteristics.

3.1.1 Expert and Expertise-Based

The traditional approach to strategy consulting assumes that consultants know more about strategy than their clients, and are therefore in the position to provide them with expert advice as to how to move forward. Clients and their employees are considered important sources of information, but it is only the consultant that can really understand what is going on with the client's strategy and that has the right expertise to offer the client proper advice. Also, because they are outsiders, consultants are able to make objective diagnoses and deliver unbiased solutions.

3.1.2 Advice-Oriented

The main aim of traditional strategy consulting is to provide the client with proper, actionable advice. This advice should be instructional and telling the client exactly what to do and why. Ideally, this advice is presented in a structured and convincing way and laid out in both a substantive report as well as an energizing presentation. While involvement in implementation is sometimes included, the advice is mostly the aspired end result of the consultant's engagement.

3.1.3 Problem-Focused

The first step and primary focus of any engagement following the traditional approach to strategy consulting is to identify an organization's key strategic problems. Organizations are seen as machines that are broken and that need to be repaired. Therefore, meticulous diagnosis and problem analysis take place to identify, categorize and prioritize the organizations main problems. As Rasiel (1999, p. 2) puts it, 'McKinsey exists to solve business problems.'

3.1.4 Project-Based

The traditional consulting approach is built around projects. Projects are specified upfront, have a demarcated scope, have a start and end point defined and an accompanying price agreed upon. They usually follow a staged approach with distinct phases such as initiation, diagnosis, solution development and closure. This project-based approach emphasizes the temporary nature of the consultants' engagement, as well as the clearly defined work or outcome that is expected from them.

3.1.5 Analytical and Structured

To diagnose problems, the traditional strategy consulting approach follows a systematic, structured analytical approach. Using tools like cause diagrams and logic trees and following the 'MECE' principle that all analyses should lead to a set of mutually exclusive and collectively exhaustive components, organizational problems are decomposed into their finest details. And then, once the root causes are identified, solutions are designed that fix the problems.

3.1.6 Hypothesis-Driven

While not all expert consultants embrace it, McKinsey works hypothesis-driven. This means that, early on in the process, consultants are stimulated to use their gut feeling and make an estimate (hypothesis) of what they think the problem and solution are. The analytical process that follows is focused on proving or disproving this hypothesis. This makes it a focused approach, which is directed towards a particular diagnosis and solution from the beginning.

3.1.7 Fact-Based and Quantitative

The traditional strategy consulting approach relies on facts. All claims that are made should be supported by qualitative and preferably quantitative data. Except for the initial hypothesis, there is little room for speculation, hunches or opinions. And emotions should be explicitly kept to the side to keep them from interfering the rational, fact-based analysis. This makes data gathering one of the most important consulting skills required, especially in the early stages of a consultant's career (Rasiel & Friga, 2001).

3.1.8 Best-Practice-Led

As mentioned in Section 2, one of the explanations of why consulting can exist is knowledge efficiencies, the idea that knowledge used at one organization can be used in other organizations as well. Strategy consultants use this for finding solutions for their diagnosed problems. Every large consulting firm has a set of generalized solutions and tools – such as the M-firm, decentralization, lay-offs or the experience curve – and a database with previous projects. Even though solutions are tailored to the specific needs of clients, their origin often lies in reusing these generalized 'best practices'.

3.1.9 Brainstorming-Based

Solutions do not only come from previously used practices. They also come from brainstorming. It is seen as 'the *sine qua non* of strategic consulting. It's what the clients really buy' because 'Let's face it. Most large, modern corporations are chock full of intelligent, knowledgeable managers who are darned good at day-to-day problem solving. McKinsey offers a new mind-set, an outsider's view that is not locked into 'the company way' of doing things' (Rasiel, 1999, p. 93). In other words, next to their expertise, it is also their creativity and outsider view that makes the expert consultant valuable.

3.1.10 Persuasive

Expert advice only works if the client can be convinced that the strategy consultant has made the right diagnosis and proposes the right solution. Therefore, persuasive communication is another hallmark of traditional strategy consulting (Clark & Fincham, 2002). McKinsey's well-known 'pyramid-style' of communication (Minto, 2009) exemplifies this, as well as the fact that the entire Part 3 of Rasiel's (1999) 'The McKinsey Way' is titled 'The McKinsey Way of *Selling* Solutions' (my emphasis) and continuously mentions the importance of generating 'buy-in'.

3.1.11 Long-Cycle and Planning-Based

With its strong emphasis on problem-solving, analysis, brainstorming and generating persuasive advice, the traditional approach to strategy consulting is based on long-cycle thinking. It dedicates a long time to cognitive work – defining the problem and the solution – before any action is taken. This means that, as is the case in traditional strategy, there is a clear divide between strategy generation and its execution and a clear focus on creating plans of which the execution takes substantial time and effort too.

3.1.12 Top Management-Focused

The most important persons for traditional strategy consulting are the client's top management. The higher in rank, the more important a person is. And usually the person highest in rank is considered to represent 'the client'. People lower in the organization are seen as potentially relevant information sources, but – at least in McKinsey's case – only if they are considered to be intelligent and open-minded enough to meet McKinsey's standards. Otherwise, they are considered liabilities to be avoided: 'There are two kinds of "liability" members on a client team: the merely useless and the actively hostile' (Rasiel, 1999, p. 129).

3.2 The Traditional Consulting Process

Along with the characterization of the traditional approach above belongs the process through which this approach is delivered. This process is mostly described along a set of steps, preferably executed in linear order. Illustrative are the following decompositions of the consulting process in steps:

• Baaij (2013): Problem diagnosis, Solution development, Solution communication, Solution implementation.

- Newton (2010): Propose to win (find, focus, frame), Deliver to satisfy (commence, collect, consider, create, counsel, consult), Close to cultivate (close).
- Rasiel and Friga (2001): Business need (competitive, organizational, financial, operational), Analysing (framing, designing, gathering, interpreting), Presenting (structure, buy-in), Managing (team, client, self), Implementation (dedication, reaction, completion, iteration), Leadership (vision, inspiration, delegation).
- Kubr (2002): Entry, Diagnosis, Action planning, Implementation, Termination.

What these descriptions of the process have in common is that they suggest a process with a clear start (e.g. Propose to win or Entry), an analytical phase in which the client's problem is diagnosed (e.g. Problem Diagnosis or Analysing), a design stage in which the solution is generated (e.g. Solution development or Action planning), a stage in which the solution is communicated (e.g. Solution communication or Presenting), an implementation stage (Solution implementation or Implementation) and a stage in which the engagement is ended (e.g. Close to cultivate or Termination). What they also have in common is that they don't distinguish between strategy consulting and other types of management consulting, implying that the same process is used for various kinds of management consulting.

While not all strategy consulting will equally fit the picture that emerges from this process and the twelve characteristics outlined in Section 3.1, it does provide a reasonably accurate description of strategy consulting as it has emerged from the historical developments summarized in the previous section. It is this approach to strategy consulting that is responsible for the majority of criticisms. Therefore, we need to look at those too.

3.3 Its Problems and Limitations

The traditional approach to strategy consulting of course has its strengths. It has always attracted some of the brightest minds and it produces meticulous analyses and persuasive advices that have put their stamp on the nature of corporations as we know them today. Furthermore, it has resulted in various powerhouses where significant money is made and which corporations feel virtually obliged to work with. But despite the success this approach has delivered consulting firms, there is broad and deep criticism too. A review of the literature shows no less than seventeen important points of criticisms raised. These are drawn both from the polemical works referred to earlier (Micklethwait & Wooldridge, 1996; O'Shea & Madigan, 1998; Pinault,

2009), as well as more balanced critiques (Clark & Fincham, 2002; Delany, 1995; Greiner et al., 2011; Kipping & Clark, 2012; McDonald, 2013; C. McKenna, 2012; McKenna, 2006; Payne & Lumsden, 1987).

3.3.1 Arrogance

There is substantial arrogance in the expert approach summarized earlier and, in particular, in its McKinsey version. Various authors have observed this and commented on how McKinsey's consultants find themselves clearly superior to their clients. Even when not having worked with them or for them, one can experience this by reading Rasiel's books and the superiority they express (Rasiel, 1999; Rasiel & Friga, 2001). While arrogance may come with other types of consulting too, it is especially present in strategy consulting, because strategy is assumed to supersede all other disciplines.

3.3.2 Pretence of Knowledge

If the observed arrogance were only a matter of style, one could argue that, even though we might not like it, strategy consultants know better than their clients and therefore have the right to be arrogant. But this is not necessarily the case. If they are experienced, strategy consultants probably know more about strategy in general then their clients. But in most cases, their clients know the specifics of their own company as well as their industry much better. And these are the specifics that matter for creating unique and sustainable value. Therefore, even though strategy consultants may possess some important knowledge, it is a best partial and incomplete.

3.3.3 Pretence of Science

One of the key mechanisms to support the pretence of knowledge is the science-inspired methods, tools and language that strategy consultants use. Cause diagrams, logic trees, hypotheses, data gathering and the MECE criteria make strategy consulting look like a scientific discipline. But much of this is rhetoric and based on a stylized image of the natural sciences. One could seriously question, for example, whether decomposing a strategic problem into components that are mutually exclusive and collectively exhaustive is useful at all. Of course, one doesn't want to overlook important aspects of a problem. But that doesn't imply that these aspects should be mutually exclusive and exhaustive. In reality they aren't. They are all interconnected and it is this interconnected nature of strategy that makes it so important.

3.3.4 Lack of Integrative View

Applying the science-inspired approach and especially the MECE criteria draws the strategy consultant's attention to details. Even though there is much talk of 'integrative views' and even though tools such as cause diagrams, logic trees and the pyramid principle should help keeping the bigger picture in mind, the emphasis is on analysing factual details. The result is that especially informal, social, intuitive and other right-brain aspects are easily overlooked because these don't lend themselves equally well to be analysed with the tools used. The holistic view these right-brain qualities can provide, though, is an essential ingredient of strategy consulting.

3.3.5 Pretence of Creativity

As referred to in Section 3.1, the consultant's creativity is assumed to be what clients really buy when hiring a strategy consultant. As outsiders, and using the brainstorming and hypothesis-driven approach, strategy consultants can come up with out-of-the box solutions that companies can't come up with themselves. This idea, though, is based on one particular view on creativity: the 'sudden spark' view that ideas must come suddenly, unexpected and from outside. A large part of creativity though, is hard work and based on cumulative previous experience. It is the people at the client's company that have this experience, not the strategy consultants.

3.3.6 Negative Orientation

The starting point for the traditional consulting approach is that something is wrong with the client's organization. Therefore, its entire focus is on repairing what is broken. Little attention is given to more appreciative approaches that build on what has been achieved and what energizes the organization. Strikingly, it is McKinsey's most famous consultant gurus Waterman and Peters who, in their book *In Search of Excellence* (Peters, Waterman, & Jones, 1982), offer an outright attack on McKinsey's problem-oriented approach (McDonald, 2013). *In Search of Excellence*, therefore, focuses on what does work instead of on problems.

3.3.7 Project Instead of Process-Based

The project-based approach to strategy consulting suggests that a clear start and end point can be defined. But that is not what strategy is like in practice. There is no start, nor is there an end. Strategy is a process that always continues because both organizations and their environment continuously evolve. And consciously or not, organizations are always in the process of executing and changing their strategies. This makes a project-based approach a mismatch with the very nature of strategy. It isolates a 'project' from the ongoing processes and thereby further reduces the integrative nature of strategy.

3.3.8 Slow and Linear

With its focus on analysis and strategy generation, traditional strategy consulting suffers from the same problem that we see in traditional strategy in general: its 'waterfall approach' is too slow and linear compared to the fast-changing world we live in and it pays too little attention to strategy execution. In a world where organizations increasingly shift to more agile, experimental and trial-and -error-based ways of working, the traditional consulting approach doesn't fit. Instead, it asks for more short-cycle iterative approaches in which implementation is integrated as part of a continuous learning cycle.

3.3.9 Disengaged

At McKinsey, a project is often called an 'engagement'. But a criticism to the traditional consulting approach is exactly that it is too disengaged. Characteristic for the traditional approach is that the strategy consultant doesn't engage much with the client. Consultants do talk to employees, but stay at a distance to keep their objective outsider view. And if they engage with employees, it is only with those that are smart enough to meet the consultant's standards to provide them with the information needed. Because making strategic changes is just as much a social process as it is analytical, this disengagement with the majority of the client's employees can make the implementation of the advice given difficult.

3.3.10 De-Humanized

Traditional strategy consulting reduces people largely to rational thinkers. People can provide or gather information, process it and communicate it. All other aspects of what makes us human beings – especially emotions – are considered a nuisance. This applies to clients, where employees are primarily seen as information sources. And it also applies to consultants. One of the hallmarks of the large consulting firms is that individual consultants are anonymous and interchangeable. Since they all meet a certain standard of intelligence and apply the consultancy's methods, it shouldn't matter which consultant is involved. Also, consultants are required to keep their subjective opinions and emotions from interfering with their work.

3.3.11 Lacking Diversity

Another, related criticism concerns the overly Caucasian masculine character of traditional consulting. Strategy consulting, as well as strategy at large, so far has a strong white male bias. This applies to the board room, academia and consulting. Even though there are various diversity and inclusion programmes, the field still has this bias – this author included. This doesn't only appear in the composition of the population of strategy consultants. It also appears in the left-brain, masculine approach to strategy consulting that was outlined earlier.

3.3.12 No Liability and Risk

The distance kept, the focus on providing advice and the fact that the responsibility for implementation is left to the client make strategy consulting a low-risk activity. Even though their advices can have major consequences for the client's organization and the people working there, strategy consultants rarely accept liability for their work. As argued before, this is one of the reasons why it doesn't qualify as a profession. This risk-free nature of strategy consulting makes that consultants can provide ineffective and even harmful advices without other consequences than not being hired again by the same client.

3.3.13 Profit-Oriented

The primary aim of traditional strategy consulting is making the client's organization more profitable, or profitable again. Often, involving strategy consultants leads to cost-cutting and lay-offs, thereby reducing the organization's yearly expenditures. And where the emphasis is on value-creation instead of cost-cutting, it targets primarily at increasing an organization's turnover. In the light of the Elkington's (1998) 'triple bottom line' of people, planet and profit, the emphasis in traditional consulting is therefore clearly on the last. In the light of the increasing attention to sustainability, this reflects a rather narrow view on the purpose of strategy consulting.

3.3.14 Self-Centred

Another criticism raised is that strategy consulting projects sometimes seem to be targeted at confirming and growing the consultant's status rather than at helping a client. Along these lines, clients must be grateful that the strategy consultant is willing to work with them and must make sure that they do everything to let the consultants do their work properly. The most important outcome in such case is not necessarily that the client is really helped, but that the consultant can close another successful project that adds to his glory and career opportunities.

3.3.15 Creating Dependence

The self-centredness is not limited to the individual consultant. Strategy consultancies (and management consultancies more generally) are also criticized for creating dependencies and lock-in effects so that the client cannot do without them anymore. Supposedly driven by greed, they are also criticized for making acquiring the next project the major aim of the current project. Such creation of lock-in and search for additional money-making opportunities is not necessarily what is best for their clients.

3.3.16 Selling Fads

Strategy consultants are also criticized for creating and selling fads rather than actually helping their clients. Through their publications, they first create feelings of anxiety at their prospective clients so that the client is receptive to a consultant's advice. Subsequently, consultants come in with their self-developed tools to solve the problem and take away the anxiety they have created themselves. As such, the criticism goes, strategy consultants are merely well-skilled salespersons and marketeers being able to sell hot air.

3.3.17 Unethical

A final and broader criticism that results from several of the above criticisms is that strategy consulting is to some extent unethical. The degree to which it is unethical obviously depends largely on the degree to which consultancies or individual consultants show the behaviours above. But as we can invoke from the amount and strong-worded arguments in the critical literature, it is a criticism that cannot be taken lightly. And in the light of the discussion about strategy consulting as a profession, it is a point of criticism that needs to be addressed adequately.

Together, these seventeen points of criticism form a broad-fronted attack of the traditional consulting approach, and particularly to how it is used by the large consulting corporations. Of course, not all criticism can be directly related to the approach as such. Part of it is aimed at the particular practice of McKinsey or even at particular cases of consulting that have received media attention. Also, in outlining the traditional approach in the previous section and providing the criticisms in this section, I used a bit of a strawman approach. Practice is more nuanced and things may not be as bad as they seem from the past sections.

Nevertheless, the criticisms are there. And they do form a coherent attack, thereby emphasizing the main limitations and weaknesses of the traditional approach to strategy consulting. This suggests that, if we want to do better in the future, strategy consulting needs to change. The next three sections offer a suggestion as to in which direction and how.

4 The Nature and Purpose of Strategy Consulting

For outlining a productive approach to strategy consulting that can withstand the critiques of the previous section, I start with identifying the nature of strategy consulting and what it should lead to in this section. Thereafter, the next two sections will zoom in on the strategy consulting process that can bring us there (Section 5) and the roles the strategy consultant plays in achieving this (Section 6).

4.1 The Nature of Strategy Consulting

In Section 1, strategy consulting was defined as helping organizations achieve unique and sustainable value creation as an external and independent professional. To better understand what this means, it is useful to have a closer look at the nature of strategy consulting. We can do this along five dimensions: exploration vs. exploitation, reductionism vs. holism, strategy generation vs. strategy execution, instrumental vs. normative and idealism vs. pragmatism.

4.1.1 Exploration vs. Exploitation

The strategy and management literature are full of references to the notions of exploration and exploitation and variations thereof. Especially in publications on ambidexterity (Birkinshaw & Gibson, 2004; O'Reilly III & Tushman, 2004; Raisch & Birkinshaw, 2008) and organizational learning (March, 1991), this distinction is made. Exploitation refers to an organization's operational activities aimed at delivering its products and services in a focused and efficient way. It creates stability. Exploration refers to innovation, developing new products and services and renewal and thereby creates flexibility. To be effective in the long run, organizations need a balanced approach in which both have their place.

Operational consulting approaches such as 'lean' or 'six sigma' focus on improving an organization's efficiency. They are exploitation-focused. Characteristic for such consulting is that projects can be clearly defined upfront and are aimed at resolving unnecessary inefficiencies in the organization. The same applies to many forms of HR, marketing, IT or financial consulting: they take the organization's strategy – its current way of value creation – as the starting point and from thereon derive what needs to be done in order to realize this strategy from an operational, HR, marketing, IT or financial perspective. This means that, in these types of consultancies, the overall goal is assumed to be largely given, making the consulting primarily about helping organizations achieving that goal.

Strategy consulting is different. Its very purpose is defining the goal that is assumed given in other types of consulting. It defines the direction of the organization in the near or far future. Therefore, strategy consulting is mostly oriented towards the explorative side of this spectrum. This means it is more open and opportunity-oriented than most other types of consulting. Rather than starting from a clear problem definition or objective, strategy consulting starts from a broader assignment to help a client identify and realize new or better ways of creating unique value.

This difference has consequences for the nature of strategy consulting. Along the lines of the criticisms of the previous section, it means that strategy consulting cannot be merely problem-focused, hypothesis-driven, best-practice-led or project-based. Because, more often than not, there is no upfront problem for which a hypothesis, best practice or project can be defined. If the strategy consultant is involved timely, there isn't even a problem at all. Instead, there are, for example, aspirations, ideas, observations and questions the client needs help with sorting out and turning into strategy and action.

4.1.2 Reductionist vs. Holistic Thinking

Another important distinction to understand strategy consulting is between reductionist thinking and holistic thinking. With reductionist thinking, one decomposes something into its finest parts in order to understand it and improve it. This works for understanding and fixing machines, inefficiencies and operational problems and it is also how most sciences work. The traditional approach to strategy consulting is a clear example of reductionist thinking. With its science and engineering-inspired cause diagrams, logic trees and MECE criteria, it does exactly what the reductionist approach tells us to do: decompose a problem into its finest parts and start solving it from thereon.

But this is not how strategy works. Strategy is integrative by its very nature and therefore requires holistic thinking. Of course, we can define the components of which strategy consists and this is even useful. I have done this too, in two earlier books (Kraaijenbrink, 2015, 2018), where I decomposed both the notions of strategy and organization into their key components. The two frameworks developed for that – the Strategy Sketch and the Organizational Map – are part of the backbone of my approach to strategy. So, I certainly believe that decomposing strategy into its constituting parts is useful. But the point of doing that is understanding strategy as an integrative whole, as a system (or *Gestalt*, as it is also called) of mutually dependent components that cannot be separated.

This means that the left-brain, science and engineering-inspired approach of unravelling problems into their finest MECE components cannot work for strategy consulting. Or at least, it means that it is severely limited and needs to be complemented by right-brain holistic thinking. Some strategy consultants may find this uncomfortable. It means departing from the analytical mindset with its safe and structured approaches and relying more loosely on intuition, understanding and judgement.

4.1.3 Strategy Generation vs. Execution

Traditional strategy consulting has a strong focus on strategy generation (or formation). Strategy execution (or implementation) is often optional and not preferred because it means getting one's hands dirty and taking more responsibility for the advice given. This means that the ideal traditional strategy consulting project ends with a convincing plan and presentation telling the client exactly what to do and why – and then leave.

There are three reasons why such approach to strategy consulting is not preferred. First, it creates an artificial watershed between strategy generation and execution (Martin, 2015). Both are part of one and the same process and by separating them, one creates a conceptual distinction that doesn't exist in practice. We see this same problem in strategy more generally and it is one of the causes of so much unrealized strategy. Since no organization needs a strategy that is not executed, strategy generation and execution always need to go hand in hand.

The second reason is that separating strategy generation and execution limits the possibilities for learning. It leads to a static, linear process during which little experimentation and learning can take place. Especially in a world as dynamic as it is today, this will mean the generated strategy is likely to be outdated even before the consultant's final presentation. When strategy generation and execution go hand in hand, however, learning and adjustment can take place on a continuous basis, leading to a strategy that is up to date and relevant on an ongoing basis.

Third, separating the two and focusing on strategy generation hinder creating commitment throughout the client's organization. In the traditional approach there is much speak of 'selling' the advice to create 'buy-in'. But buy-in is not real commitment. Next to the fact that it is usually only targeted at the client's management, buy-in aims at changing people's minds so that they believe you and do as you suggested. Commitment, though, means feeling responsible for making something work that you believe in. This requires participation by those involved in execution.

4.1.4 Instrumental vs. Normative

A fourth dimension that is key to strategy consulting is that of instrumental vs. normative consulting. Instrumental consulting accepts the client's values and goals as given and helps the client achieve them. The consulting is instrumental because it doesn't question the client's values and goals. It takes them as given 'norms' and only concerns how to realize them. With normative consulting, on the other hand, the consultant is also involved in defining proper values and goals for the client. This involves bringing in moral and ethical judgements and methods to help the client decide about the right values and goals for the organization.

No consulting is value and norm free. By interacting with clients, consultants always bring in their own normative views, consciously or unconsciously. This means that there are instrumental and normative elements in every type of consultancy. The normative element, though, is especially relevant in strategy consulting. As referred in in Section 4.1.1, strategy consulting is about helping a client define the organization's aspired directions. This includes defining the key values and goals that should guide the organization – including its vision, mission and key values, should we want to adopt these traditional starting points of strategy. Since these depend on what is held as desirable, they are derived from the normative frameworks of those involved.

The tension between instrumental and normative aspects of consulting can be challenging for strategy consultants. On the one hand, they could simply accept the client's values and goals and help them instrumentally achieve those. However, if strategy consulting is to be more like a profession, this is not enough. If the client has questionable values and goals that may harm particular groups of stakeholders or society at large, it is also the strategy consultant's professional responsibility to help client's reconsider and adjust them in a more favourable direction.

4.1.5 Idealism vs. Pragmatism

The previous two dimensions – strategy generation vs. execution and instrumental vs. normative – imply a fifth one: idealism vs. pragmatism. On the one hand, as a strategy consultant, one reaches for the ideal: that strategy that, if realized, would help the organization make a substantial step forward in the value it creates. In such case, strategy generation and a normative approach to consulting may be given most weight. On the other hand, though, one must also keep in mind what is realistic and what can practically be achieved. In such case, strategy execution and instrumentalism are given most weight.

Both are needed. Without idealism, strategy consulting is merely an instrumental job and nothing close to a profession. But without pragmatism, it is largely a fantasy or feel-good exercise without actual impact on the client's organization. This means that, as a strategy consultant, one always needs to find a balance between the two. Along the idea that 'a mediocre strategy well executed is better than a great strategy poorly executed', some argue that pragmatism is more important than idealism. But for strategy consulting this is too weak. Of course, a great strategy that is not executed is of little use to the organization. However, helping the client execute a mediocre or questionable strategy is of little use too. For generating and executing such strategies, organizations don't need strategy consultants. They are hired to come up with something that is better than mediocre or questionable.

In their work on strategy making, Ackermann and Eden (2011) refer to the tension between idealism and pragmatism by arguing that strategy needs both to be analytically sound and politically feasible. A strategy is analytically sound if it is a good strategy on paper; a strategy that makes sense; and that, if executed, should help the organization forward. This reflects the idealistic dimension. A strategy is politically feasible when people in the organization feel capable and committed to execute the strategy. Following their line of reasoning and using Rumelt's (2011) terminology, a 'good' strategy is one that combines idealism with pragmatism.

4.2 The Client and Their Needs

While it is common in most industries to speak of customers, consultants usually speak of clients. Following this habit, I also use the word client throughout this Element. To identify the purpose of strategy consulting, we first need to get clarity on who the client is and what it is that the client needs.

4.2.1 Who Is the Client?

Identifying the client's needs starts with defining who actually the client is. This is not a trivial question and there are multiple possible answers to this:

1. **A single stakeholder:** this is usually the person highest in rank with executive responsibility for the unit or organization that requires consulting (e.g. the CEO). It is also the person responsible for the budget from which the consultant is being paid.

2. **Multiple stakeholders:** one can also follow a multi-stakeholder approach and consider more than one group as clients. Typical stakeholders include management, the board and employees. Each group has specific needs and stakes that are to be addressed.
3. **The organization:** one can also define the organization as a whole as the client. This means abstracting from specific persons and targeting the consulting at what is best for the survival and prosperity of the organization.
4. **Society:** taking an even broader view one can also see society as key client. This means looking at the economic, social and environmental impact of the organization and aiming the consulting at improving this impact. In such case, societal needs direct the consulting work.

In the traditional approach, the client is typically a single stakeholder: the CEO or another executive high in rank. This doesn't mean that other stakeholders are not considered. It means that this one stakeholder is considered to be the primary stakeholder that needs to be satisfied and convinced of the final advice. A key reason is that it is this stakeholder who decides on whether or not the consultant's invoice is being paid. Therefore, satisfying their needs is more important than satisfying the needs of other stakeholders.

Despite the wide usage of the single-stakeholder approach, I want to make the case for the third option: seeing the organization rather than one or more specific types of stakeholder as primary client. This is the approach I use in my own consulting and arguably more effective in today's dynamic and complex world (Greiner et al., 2011). The reason to prefer it above the first approach is twofold. First, it is the organization that needs strategy, not the CEO or any other particular stakeholder. While any particular stakeholder might recognize the need and express it, one generates strategy for the organization as a whole and it is the organization that needs to execute it. This means that taking the organization as primary client increases the likelihood that the strategy consulting services given will be relevant.

A second reason is that taking the organization rather than any particular stakeholder as client fosters consulting that is ethical and value-added for society. It reduces the chances of being used as a consultant for the personal benefit of a particular stakeholder. Accordingly, considering the organization as client helps moving strategy consulting forward to becoming a profession. Not in a top-down fashion through installing institutions, but bottom-up through adopting an approach that makes ethical and value-added consulting more likely.

Even though taking society as primary client is possible too, I consider it too far on the normative and idealist side in terms of the dimensions distinguished earlier. At the end, the strategy consultant is hired and paid by the client's organization. This implies that their primary duty is to serve them, not society as a whole. However, by applying proper ethical standards, focusing the consulting on sustainable value creation and adopting a whole-person approach, societal needs are automatically addressed in an indirect way. This means that by taking the organization as primary client, the approach outlined in this Element contributes to society as well.

As I can tell from personal experience, treating the organization as primary client is not always easy. It becomes particularly challenging if the person holding the budget for paying you, for example the CEO, is a problem for the organization. They are usually highly involved in strategy and, consequently, it is not exceptional that they are also to a large extent the cause of bad or ineffective strategy. This leads to interesting dilemmas that require smart navigation between idealism (doing what is good for the organization) and pragmatism (keep a good enough relationship with the respective executive). But there are always dilemmas. Therefore, following Greiner, Motamedi, and Jamieson's (2011) advice, the preferred approach for strategy consulting is considering the organization rather than a single stakeholder as primary client.

4.2.2 What Do They Need?

Taking the organization as primary client rather than a specific person or group of persons makes understanding their needs slightly more challenging than usual. Being an abstract entity, an organization has strictly spoken no needs. Only living creatures have needs. This means that these are the organization's people who have needs. And given their various backgrounds and responsibilities, people's specific needs will differ. But this is a problem that exists for every business-to-business service where the client is an organization. And it is only a problem as far as we follow a reductionist approach and aim at defining an exhaustive list of specific needs of a specific stakeholder. At a more holistic level, though, we can speak of an organization's needs without any problems.

Organizations have perceived needs and real needs. Perceived needs refer to what clients think they need. When they hire a strategy consultant, it is likely they think they need a new or adjusted strategy. And what they might have in mind, based on the conventional ideas about what strategy is, is a written strategic plan for the next three to five years. But, unless it is to convince a financier, that is rarely what they really need. In fact, no organization needs a strategy per se. Formulating one can be an intermediate step, but what the client really needs are actual changes. Changes in how the market is approached, changes in the organization's structure or resource-base, changes in the financial structure, and so on. It is always the factual change that is the real need. This means the client's perceived needs and their actual needs may differ substantially and that it is the consultant's job to make the client realize this and to take both into account.

It is also useful to recognize that the client has both functional needs and emotional needs. Functional needs are strategy and organization-related needs: in their search for more unique and sustainable value creation, organizations need support to identify and realize opportunities for improvement. These needs refer to the contents of strategy and most of the traditional consulting approach focuses on these needs. Emotional needs, on the other hand, refer to how people in the organization feel and how they want to feel. Given the limited attention given to these needs in most of the consulting literature (Maister, Green, and Galford (2000) being a notable exception), it is worth listing them. Clients may feel:

- Concerned, worried about the future of the organization and its employees.
- Uncertain, insecure and lacking ideas and confidence about the next steps to take.
- Afraid of what is going to come, of failing, of taking risk or making the wrong decision.
- Overwhelmed, stressed and busy, not being able to take time for strategy.
- Threatened by their superiors, competitors or the world around them more generally.
- Incapable, lacking strategic skills and expertise, ignorant.
- Impatient, fed up with lack of progress, glad to finally get started.
- Sceptical, suspicious about whether consulting is going to help.
- Curious, eager to learn new perspectives and receive new insights and information.

Most clients will not advertise these feelings. That would make them look vulnerable and weak, they may think. But recognizing these feelings is key to successful consulting. While the functional, content-oriented part of strategy consulting is of course important, the emotional part is at least as important. At the bottom-line, clients want peace of mind. They want their negative feelings be resolved and be confident that they are doing the right thing to make their organization survive and prosper. Without addressing such emotional needs, one could develop a great strategy but that is never implemented because people's emotions haven't changed.

4.3 What Strategy Consulting Should Lead To

Having described the nature of strategy consulting and the general needs clients have, we can now turn to the targeted outcomes of strategy consulting. These are not analyses, models, plans, projections, PowerPoint decks or presentations. Those are means at best and neither necessary nor sufficient. In defining what strategy consulting then should lead to, we can distinguish between short-term and long-term outcomes.

4.3.1 Short-Term Outcomes

At its core, the targeted short-term outcomes of strategy consulting are shared insights, endorsed decisions and committed actions about what is, what might be, what should be and what will be. The first three refer to the type of outcomes that strategy consulting should lead to:

- **Shared insights** means that people in the organization develop a common understanding of those things that matter most. This doesn't mean they all have to agree 100 percent. It means that they speak the same language and that they mostly agree on most of the facts that matter. This is key because it creates mental alignment in the organization, leading to everyone being 'on the same page' when it concerns the organization's strategy.
- **Endorsed decisions** means that the choices and decisions being made are approved or at least accepted by the people in the organization. In strategy there is no absolute right or wrong and since it concerns the future, there is no certainty about any decision. But if decisions are widely and preferably publicly supported by people throughout the organization, this increases the likelihood of a strategy being embraced and successfully executed.
- **Committed actions** means that people know what needs to be done and are willing to do that. It also means that it is not only clear what needs to be done, but also whose task it is to do it. Even further, it means that people feel responsible themselves for doing it and see it as their job, or even their pride, to do it successfully. Such commitment is key to the success execution of strategy.

With these three as main types of outcomes of strategy consulting, we can immediately see that strategy consulting is not merely about giving organizations a strategy or strategic advice. It is about leading and helping the organization towards shared insights, endorsed decisions and committed actions about how to create unique and sustainable value.

The insights, decisions and actions that are generated are always about something. Generally, and along the definition of strategy given, they are about how the organization can improve its unique way of sustainable value creation. But this overall purpose can be divided into four questions that strategy consulting should help answering:

- **What *is***: the first question strategy consulting can help answering is creating a shared understanding of what the current, factual strategy of the organization is. A thorough understanding of how things currently are – the *status quo* – needed as basis for any further strategizing. It provides a foundation on which future strategy can rely.

- **What *might* be**: strategy consulting also can help elicit pre-existing ideas, generate new ones and open people's eyes about what could or might be. Also, strategy consultants can bring in their own ideas and perspectives on the future of the organization. As such, they can help envisioning one or more inspiring and attractive scenarios for the future.

- **What *should* be**: there is also a role for the strategy consultant to help the client define what the new or improved strategy should look like. In this, the consultant can help the client define goals, values and criteria for the organization's strategy and thereby facilitate making the right choices – instrumentally and normatively.

- **What *will* be**: whereas the first question is factual and the second and third are hypothetical, in this fourth question the consultant helps the client make choices about what the new or improved strategy is going to be. This involves making the shift towards actually making decisions and committing to making changes.

The reader familiar with appreciative inquiry will recognize its four-step approach of discovery, dream, design and destiny (Cooperrider & Srivastva, 1987; Whitney & Cooperrider, 2005) in these four questions. Listing the four questions above does not imply that a full appreciative inquiry approach is required. What it implies is that these are the fundamental questions the strategy consultant needs to help the client achieve shared insights, endorsed decisions and committed actions about.

4.3.2 Long-Term Outcomes

Next to these short-term, direct outcomes of strategy consulting, I believe that strategy consulting should also aim for a more fundamental, long-term outcome: building strategic capability – the ability to effectively generate and execute strategy. In the light of what is known about core competencies (Prahalad & Hamel, 1990) and dynamic capabilities (Teece, Pisano, & Shuen, 1997), it is striking that many organizations hire strategy consultants. It shows that organizations lack sufficient strategic capability themselves. Strategy consulting can help solve this crucial void.

We live in a time where the possibilities of generating a sustainable competitive advantage are limited. Over the past decades, the thoughts about how to achieve it have shifted from resources (Barney, 1991) to dynamic capabilities (Teece et al., 1997) to the idea that no such sustainable advantage can exist (McGrath, 2013). However, if there is any capability that can give an organization a competitive advantage today, it is the capability to effectively generate and execute strategy. Organizations that have this capability have an effective process in place for generating and executing strategy on an ongoing basis. This enables them to seize opportunities and respond strategically to internal and external changes. It also enables them to adjust their strategy when needed and keep the execution aligned with it.

Strategy consulting can help organizations develop that capability. Through engaging with the consultant, the client learns how to strategize by doing it. Initially they may require the full supervision of the consultant. But once they have gone through the process multiple times, they will be increasingly able to do it themselves, thereby gradually taking ownership over the process back from the consultant and thereby gradually improving their strategic capability.

This outcome cannot be achieved with the traditional consulting approach. Being an expert approach, it relies on the information asymmetry between client and consultant and on the very fact that the client should remain dependent on the consultant. Furthermore, when clients develop strategic capability themselves, this reduces the need for traditional, expert consulting. This means there is a direct incentive in traditional consulting to make sure that the client does not develop a too strong strategic capability.

Through the more engaged and co-constructive approach to strategy consulting outlined in this Element, clients are actively involved and thereby will learn by doing. At its core, the process as it is outlined in the next section is a participative process where the consultant and the client work side by side on a better strategy for the organization. Throughout this process, people throughout the organization will develop a better understanding of what the organization's strategy is, what it could be, what it should be and what it will be.

5 The Strategy Consulting Process

After having given a description of what strategy consulting is like and what it should lead to in the previous sections, this section gets to its heart: the strategy consulting process. In describing this process, this Element only covers the actual consulting process. This means, for example, that selling and negotiating a project are not covered. Those steps are explained extensively elsewhere (Baaij, 2013; Block, 2000) and are similar for strategy consulting than for other types of consulting. To create a solid understanding of the strategy consulting process, this section first characterizes the nature of the process as a whole and then describes the parts it consists of.

5.1 The Nature of the Process

The previous sections already provide us with a high-level idea what the strategy consulting process looks like. We have seen, for example, the traditional approach and its criticisms and the kind of outcomes strategy consulting should lead to. This makes it evident that the process is not as analytical, science-inspired, problem-focused, linear and project-based as traditionally suggested. And, as already anticipated in Section 1.4, the approach outlined in this Element is a whole-brain, whole-person approach to strategy consulting. This leads to the following high-level characterization of the strategy consulting process:

1. **Co-constructive:** both the client and the consultant have key expertise that they bring in the process. None of them is the ultimate expert and both learn from the other. The consultant doesn't offer and sell a strategic advice to the client. Together, they create a shared understanding, endorsed decisions and committed actions that should help move the organization forward.

2. **Intersubjective**: implied by the previous, but worthwhile mentioning separately, there are no objective truths in strategy. The best that can be achieved is agreement between people. Purely subjective opinions are no basis either, but through a co-constructive approach, intersubjective ideas emerge regarding all four questions referred to earlier.

3. **Iterative**: because any idea about the future is speculative and most likely wrong, strategy consulting needs to rely on a short-cycle approach in which ideas are put to the test. This means that strategy generation and execution go hand in hand and that the process is flexible and open to new insights and opportunities.

4. **Participative**: since the organization as a whole is affected by strategy and involved in the execution, strategy consulting needs to be a participative process in which many or even all employees are involved at some point of time. Not merely as sources of information, but as change agents within their own sphere of influence.

5. **Appreciative**: if they hinder progress, problems need to be resolved. But problems don't energize people and an organization's weaknesses are no good basis for strategy. Therefore, the focus is on searching for the best in people, the organization and the environment. With that focus, problems will be easier to resolve too.

6. **Integrative**: a key purpose of strategy is that it creates alignment so that all, or at least most, energy is used in the same direction. Therefore, strategy consulting should foster integration and alignment of all parts of the organization. This implies always keeping the whole picture in mind and also bringing people closer together.

7. **Social**: because strategy consulting induces changes in people's roles and relationships, the process is inherently social. Of course, identifying a fruitful direction for the organization is important, but it is the people that need to get there. This applies to the execution, but also to the generation of strategy: both parts of the process are social.

8. **Continuous**: even though the consultant's actual involvement may be only temporary, strategy consulting needs to take place from a continuous perspective on the strategy process. The consultant joins a running organization for a while and can help direct it to a better destination. But unlike in a project, there is no start and end point.

9. **Non-sequential**: the process is non-linear. Not only by its iterative nature, but also because its parts or steps run in parallel. There is a logical sequence in which things are theoretically done. But, as we will see later, to a large extent, things are done in parallel and require attention throughout the process.

As can be inferred from these nine characteristics, the strategy process suggested here differs substantially and quite fundamentally from the traditional approach. As we will see in the next section and the remainder of this Element, this has consequences for what the steps the process is comprised of as well as for the roles the strategy consultant plays in this process.

5.2 Parts of the Process

The characteristics described earlier imply that the strategy consulting process is not as linear and strictly phased as sometimes suggested. It rather is an ongoing process in which various activities are performed in parallel. Nevertheless, we can distinguish the main activities of which the process is comprised. These can be divided into three groups: establishing context, generating strategy and executing strategy. They are visualized in Figure 1 and explained below.

5.2.1 Establishing Context

The first set of activities in consulting – strategy and other types – is making sure that the right context is in place for effective consulting. Without the right context, strategy consulting will not lead to satisfying results for the client and the consultant. Six types of activities can be distinguished.

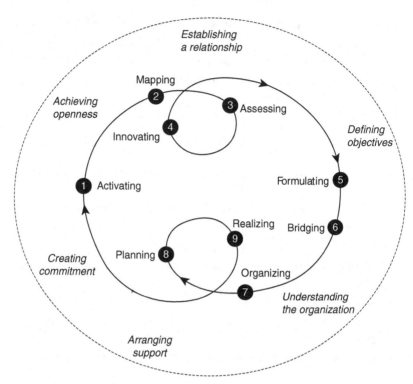

Figure 1 The strategy consulting process

Establishing and Maintaining a Good Relationship

Consulting is first and foremost a people process. A consultant talks to people, listens to them and guides them in a particular direction. Doing this effectively requires a good relationship with the client. Not just with the CEO, but with people throughout the organization. The consultant doesn't need to be their best friend, but, as research by for example Cialdini (2006) shows, one can achieve much more if people like you. Therefore, an essential part of the consulting job is to establish a good relationship and actively maintain this relationship throughout the process.

Defining and Redefining the Task and Objective

Also crucial for effective consulting is agreeing on what the consultant and the client are aiming to achieve and what the consultant's role will be in that. In the traditional approach, this is defined upfront and turned into a clearly demarcated project and planning. While it is necessary to manage mutual expectations upfront, strategy is often too explorative, continuous and dynamic to define everything in advance. Therefore, to acknowledge this nature of strategy, the definition of tasks and objectives is best seen as a continuous, iterative process in which both are adjusted and redefined when new insights emerge.

Understanding How the Organization Works

Every organization has its own particular structure, culture, habits and language (Spender, 2014). To be effective, a strategy consultant needs to understand how the client's organization works. This includes understanding how communication takes place, which relationships there are between units, who is in power, how formal or informal the organization is and how the organization and strategy have emerged over the last few years. This is not meant as a diagnosis or problem analysis. It is a necessary step for understanding how, as a consultant, one should act and what one should and should not say and do. Since, throughout the strategy consulting process new information will appear, getting to know the organization is, like the previous activities, an ongoing process.

Checking and Arranging Support and Resources

Strategy consultants cannot work in isolation. Their goal is to help the client's organization change. This means that they need to be in a position in which they can achieve that. For that it is necessary that the support and resources needed to achieve the tasks and objectives agreed upon are available. This includes that there is sufficient budget and manpower available for the process and that the consultant has access to the information that is needed. It also includes obtaining the necessary mandate and freedom to operate. Given that the direction of the process may change repeatedly, also this fourth type of activity requires attention throughout the process.

Creating Commitment and Engagement

No matter how great is the strategy that the consultant and client create together, it will only lead to the aspired changes if there is sufficient commitment and engagement by the people that are affected. Commitment means that people feel responsible for doing what is needed and engagement means that they actively participate and contribute during the process. Because both take time to develop, strategy consultants need to work on creating commitment and engagement from the earliest phases on and continuously throughout the process. This means involving people, listening to them, informing them regularly and taking their contributions seriously.

Achieving Openness and Transparency

Strategy consulting is most effective when it addresses the things that really matter in the organization. Given the importance and complexity of the topic and its potential impact, there may be important issues involved that don't get immediately on the table. Often these concern the quality of leaders, a lack of trust or an unwillingness to talk about the real issues going on. This may lead to elephants in the room that hinder significant process. Since the strategy consultant's aim is to help the organization, part of their task is to identify these elephants, name them and create an atmosphere in which people are willing to talk about them.

All six activities are particularly important in the early phases of an engagement, but they stay important throughout the entire process. Both the context and the emerging new or adjusted strategy will change. Particularly in complex situations where change is dramatic or tensions are present, these six types of activities require constant attention.

5.2.2 Setting Direction: Generating Strategy

The second type of activities are those that are traditionally seen as the heart of strategy consulting: generating strategy. Unlike the traditional approach, though, this doesn't refer to generating strategy *for* the organization. It refers to generating strategy *with* them, through an interactive, co-creative process. This means the consultant joins the client in the strategy generation process. Since I have described this process extensively in *The Strategy Handbook* (Kraaijenbrink, 2015), I will adopt the five steps explained there and summarize them briefly.

Step 1: Activating key stakeholders. *Making key persons in the organization receptive to new strategy and mobilizing the resources needed for strategy generation.*

This first step resides at the intersection between establishing context and generating strategy. The fact that a strategy consultant is hired, shows that there is at least one influential person in the organization convinced that the organization's strategy requires attention. This certainly doesn't mean, however, that others think alike. This can mean that some of the very first activities of the consultant need to be creating awareness and motivating people in the organization to actively commit and engage in the strategy making process. This includes making sure that the right people are present in the team(s) the consultant works with and getting those people on board to actively contribute.

Step 2: Mapping strategy. *Identifying the organization's strategy by describing it on the basis of its core elements.*

To effectively generate a new or improved strategy that suits the organization, the next step is developing a thorough understanding of the organization's status quo; its current, factual strategy. As an outsider, the consultant needs this to understand the organization and where it is going. But also internally, this step serves an important purpose: it generates a shared point of reference and understanding of what the current strategy of the organization actually is. For most people involved, this may be the very first time they talk explicitly about their organization's strategy. As such, this step forms the beginning of a productive dialogue.

As the definition of this step above hints at, the suggested way of doing this is to open up the black box of strategy and describe its elements at a relatively fine level of detail. There are various frameworks that can be used for this, including Hambrick and Fredrickson's (2001) 'Five Major Elements of Strategy' or the popular 'Business Model Canvas' (Osterwalder & Pigneur, 2010). In my own consulting I use the 'Strategy Sketch' (Kraaijenbrink, 2015), a framework containing the ten key elements of strategy: value proposition, customers and needs, competitors, resources and competencies, partners, revenue model, risks and costs, values and goals, organizational climate and trends and uncertainties. This framework builds on the Business Model Canvas, but provides a more systematic and complete view on the elements of which strategy is composed.

Using detailed frameworks like these has three important benefits. First, it creates a shared language and visualization making clear what strategy is about. Second, it allows people throughout the organization to participate, even if they have no experience or knowledge of strategy at all. Third, it makes the dialogue concrete and thereby more actionable than a high-level discussion about, for example, generic strategies (Porter, 1980) or an organization's 'why' (Sinek, 2009).

Step 3: Assessing strategy. *Judging and testing the quality of the organization's strategy against relevant criteria.*

Step 2 aimed at creating shared understanding. As such, it is mostly descriptive. To move forward and improve the organization's strategy, the third step is to assess it against a set of agreed upon criteria. Traditionally this is done in the SWOT analysis – to identify the organization's strengths, weaknesses, opportunities and threats. When distinguishing the positive aspects of strategy (strengths and opportunities) from the negative ones (weaknesses and threats), though, one implicitly or explicitly uses criteria in making a judgement. To make the assessment as objective as possible, it is useful to make these criteria explicit. The literature provides various criteria for this, of which we can compile the following list: coherence, efficiency, effectiveness, uniqueness, flexibility, robustness, scalability and responsibility (Kraaijenbrink, 2015).

The advantage of separating the assessment step from mapping is that it helps clarifying whether one is merely describing the status quo or assessing it against a normative framework. This makes the judgement more transparent and less subjective. It also makes that, during the mapping step, the focus is on understanding how things are without interference by ideas about how things should be. Furthermore, separating the assessment step from the mapping step also enables performing another assessment of the newly generated or improved strategy after the next step in the process. It fosters an iterative process in which the steps follow each other in short cycles.

Step 4: Innovating strategy. *Renewing and redesigning the organization's strategy through incremental or radical innovation.*

Steps 2 and 3 provide important input for developing a new or improved strategy. They show where problems are, which aspirations exist and on which strengths the organization can build. This, though, does not automatically lead to a new strategy. An additional, more creative and design-oriented step is needed in which the consultant, together with the organization, redesigns the organization's strategy. Various approaches can be used for this, including 'Blue Ocean Strategy' (Kim & Mauborgne, 2005), scenario planning (Schoemaker, 1995) or design thinking (Brown, 2008).

Applying one or more of these techniques and the previous steps leads to one or more points of departure for the new strategy. This could be a valuable resource, a market opportunity, a creative idea, a substantial problem, a particular aspiration, or anything else. Starting from those points of departure, the consultant can help the organization develop a complete strategy along all the elements of the framework used in Step 2. In my own case, this means that, together with the client, we redesign the strategy along all ten elements of the Strategy Sketch.

Step 5: Formulating strategy. *Capturing the organization's strategy in words and pictures that can be understood by the target audience.*

Once the strategy is redesigned, it also needs to be formulated. This doesn't imply extensive documents or presentations. It can also be a PowerPoint slide, a sheet of paper, a brochure or a picture. Formulating strategy is an essential step, as a strategy can only be effective if it can be formulated in a clear and comprehensible manner so that people can understand it and act upon it. Furthermore, formulating strategy also helps discover unclarities in the strategy that may have remained below the surface in the previous steps. Finally, turning the developed strategy into a convincing formulation can motivate and direct people's attitudes and behaviours.

This fifth step forms a temporary closure of the strategy generation process. As explained earlier, strategy generation and execution are ongoing processes that are inextricably linked and between which the organization has to go back and forth. However, at some point in time, one needs to stop generating new ideas and focus on their execution.

5.2.3 Realizing Change: Executing Strategy

The third group of activities in strategy consulting are focused on realizing actual change through executing the developed or emerging strategy. Even though strategy generation and execution are closely linked, they can be separated conceptually. Furthermore, as evidenced by the fact that the strategy consultant's engagement often ends after Step 5, in practice strategy generation and execution are often considered distinct. If the strategy consultant is truly involved in the organization's strategy process, the engagement includes activities related to strategy execution too. This involves additional steps. Once more I draw on *The Strategy Handbook* (Kraaijenbrink, 2018), because it describes in detail how I help my clients execute strategy. Four additional steps are involved.

Step 6: Bridging gaps. *Identifying the gaps between the organization's current and aspired strategy, and defining projects and tasks to bridge them.*

At any point in time there are voids between the organization's aspired strategy (resulting from Step 4) and its status quo (resulting from Step 2). The first step in executing the new, aspired strategy is to make these voids explicit and define actions to resolve them. Here the advantage of the detailed and structured approach of using a single framework such as the Strategy Sketch for describing both the status quo and the aspired strategy appears again. Comparing both on each of the elements of the framework, is a straightforward activity and it directly facilitates formulating projects and tasks that can bridge these gaps.

Step 7: Organizing strategy. *Identifying the most important organizational deficiencies, and defining projects and tasks to solve them.*

The projects and tasks defined in the previous step are not sufficient to successfully execute the strategy. It will also require organizational changes, for example, in the organization's structure, incentive systems, communication or processes. Step 7 aims at identifying these required changes and define actions to achieve them – through the same collaborative process as described earlier.

Like in the previous steps, it is helpful to use a structured framework that identifies the main components of 'organization'. The most well-known framework for this is McKinsey's 7S model, developed by Waterman and colleagues in the early 1980s (Waterman, 1982; Waterman, Peters, & Phillips, 1980). In my own consulting work I prefer the more recent and complete 'Organizational Map' (Kraaijenbrink, 2018), which contains the ten key elements of organization: leadership, controls, motivation, commitment, expertise, information technology, structure, communication, processes and policies. For each of these elements, the consultant and client can together identify which changes are needed in order to execute the strategy successfully.

Step 8: Planning strategy. *Developing and committing to a dynamic, prioritized course of action and a way of working for closing the gap between the actual and the aspired strategy.*

Up to this step, the newly developed strategy and the identified actions needed for executing it are still largely hypothetical. Together with the client, the consultant has identified what *is* (Steps 1, 2 and 3), what *could be* (Step 4) and what *should be* (Steps 5, 6 and 7). Through the transparent co-creative process, people have been engaged. This normally will have increased their willingness to execute as well. However, no actual commitment has been asked yet. This changes in Step 8, where a transition is made from the hypothetical *is, could be* and *should be*, to the actual *will be*. This includes helping the client decide about which actions have most priority, when to execute them, how many resources to dedicate and who will be responsible.

The importance of the different nature of this eighth step can hardly be overestimated. It is in this step that the consequences of the new strategy become real. Consequently, it is also in this step that resistance to change tends to be strongest. The comprehensiveness and participative nature of the previous steps help reducing resistance as much as possible. But given that strategy virtually always implies substantial changes, there will remain resistance. And that resistance is most likely to uncover in this step. It goes beyond the scope of this Element to discuss in detail how to deal with resistance. But there are various valuable contributions in the change management literature about this (Ford & Ford, 2010; Ford, Ford, & D'Amelio, 2008) and also elsewhere I have expanded on this in the context of strategy execution (Kraaijenbrink, 2018).

Step 9: Realizing strategy. *Effecting the aspired strategy by putting the execution plan into action and managing relevance, progress and emotions over time.*

While the actual execution may be largely left to the client's organization and while the strategy consultant's engagement often tends to end when the realization phase is reached, strategy consultants can play an important role in this last step too. In its most engaged form, they might serve as an *ad interim* manager who is responsible for overseeing the overall progress and receive the client's mandate to actively manage the process. In that case, however, the client stays dependent on the strategy consultant, which is not in its interest in the long run. If, as suggested in Section 4, the long-term purpose of strategy consulting is helping the client's organization improve their strategic capability, a more detached form of engagement during the realization phase is preferred. This means that the primary responsibilities for executing the strategy reside at the people within the organization. The strategy consultant can serve as a mentor and monitor who keeps an eye on whether the organization is still doing what is relevant, whether sufficient progress is made, and whether the mood in the organization remains favourable.

As depicted in Figure 1, the strategy process is a continuous process in which organizations are always engaged in one way or the other. This means that the strategy consultant's role is to help the organization move forward with that process – in one or few steps, or the entire process altogether. As the figure also shows, there is not just a single cycle, but three: for strategy generation, for strategy execution and for the overall process. The reason is twofold. First, making iterations during strategy generation is usually simpler and less expensive than in strategy execution. Therefore, through piloting and testing, one wants to maximize the likelihood that the newly generated strategy is the right one and feasible. Second, during execution, one doesn't immediately question the strategy if things don't work out according to plan. The first thing to do is to define alternative actions and find different ways of achieving the aspired strategy. Only when that doesn't work, one may need to go back to the drawing board and engage in a phase of strategy generation again.

The process outlined here deviates in various ways from that of the traditional consulting approach summarized in Section 3.2: it has all the characteristics outlined in Section 5.1 and it is also more detailed and strategy-specific. With this three-cycle process, the strategy consultant can help the client generate and execute strategy in an effective and efficient way, while staying open to unexpected outcomes, changes and opportunities. How they can do this and what this means for the roles and capabilities they need in this process, is covered in the next section.

6 Strategy Consulting Roles

As can be inferred from the previous sections, a good strategy consultant needs a broad repertoire of capabilities and plays a variety of roles. Not only do they need to understand strategy and the strategy process, but they also need to be able to understand the client's organization, collaborate with the people working there, and balance short-term and long-term purpose and outcomes. To see more precisely what is needed, this section explains nine roles strategy consultants need to play and thereby what skills they need.

6.1 Attentive Listener

One of the most crucial roles and skills needed for a strategy consultant is being an attentive listener. Throughout the process, the strategy consultant needs to keep a close eye and ear on what is happening, and on what is being said and not said. The first and obvious reason is that, through attentive listening, the strategy consultant receives important information about the organization, its strategy, its aspirations, its problems and so on. A second and equally important reason, though, is that listening attentively gives people the feeling that what they say matters – and thereby that they matter. This is crucial for getting and keeping them engaged and committed throughout the process and therefore for achieving results.

Attentive listening requires an ability to create a safe environment in which people dare, or even want to speak out. In that sense, being a strategy consultant is sometimes not too far from being a psychiatrist. In my experience, most people want to speak out, especially if it concerns their aspirations and frustrations. As Maister, Green, and Galford (2000) emphasize in their book *The Trusted Advisor*, this means building trust. Like with a psychiatrist, this doesn't require building a strong personal relationship, nor does it have to take long. If one comes in with a genuine intention to help – and to listen – trust can be built in a matter of minutes.

Listening also implies staying silent and let people do the talking. A consultant needs to ask questions, but the main goal is to trigger people in the organization to tell what they want or need to tell. This often means resisting the temptation to respond or to ask another question. Simply waiting may be enough for people to continue their stories. What I have often experienced in interviews is that after about half an hour, there can be a turning point. Whilst they may politely respond to your questions initially, I have repeatedly experienced a point where people said something like 'okay … if I can really say everything, then I I'd also like to tell you that . . .' That is usually the point where the most valuable information is given.

6.2 Principal Investigator

Being a strategy consultant also requires being a strong researcher. This is widely acknowledged in the traditional consulting approach and the reason junior consultants oftentimes are involved only in doing research in the early stages of their careers. While doing research can also be an important part of the approach to strategy consulting outlined in this Element, the strategy consultant's role is somewhat different than in the traditional approach.

Because of the intersubjective, co-creative and participative nature of the approach, there is less focus on plain data gathering. For effective strategy consulting one rarely needs meticulous details about the company – not even about its financials. Some high-level data are often enough to create an understanding of the size and situation of the organization. But for the rest, most information will come from the people working at the organization and will include their views, insights and judgements.

This means that the primary skill needed is not that of the researcher who gathers information, but that of principal investigator who listens to what people in the company have to say, interprets this, connects the dots and draws conclusions – in cooperation with the client. The consultant's role is to see connections and generate insights that people in the company may not see and then to make them see these too.

6.3 Discussion Leader

One of the primary forms in which strategy consulting takes place in the approach outlined is through interactive sessions with people from the client's organization. Each step of the process may consist of one or more sessions or workshops in which the strategy consultant works with a group of people to elicit their views and co-create the new or improved strategy. Along the lines of the steps outlined in Section 5.2, this means that during these sessions, insights are generated about what is, what could be, what should be and what will be the organization's strategy.

With interactive sessions being one of the primary working forms, another important role for the strategy consultant is that of discussion leader – or facilitator or moderator as it is also called. During the sessions, the strategy consultant's role is to foster a productive dialogue and make sure that people contribute, say what they want to say, listen to each other and generate insights and decisions in a collaborative way. This implies making sure that the sessions are constructive and involve everyone present and that they don't result in disputes or people taking sides.

It also implies paying careful attention to people who are not saying what they want to say and give them the opportunity to speak out too. It happens frequently that one or more people in the room remain largely silent. Sometimes their facial expressions and gestures show that they actually want to say something, but nevertheless they don't. It is the task of the strategy consultant to either make them feel confident enough to speak out during the session, or, should that not work, to listen to what they have to say outside the sessions.

6.4 Critical Inspirator

The first three roles are largely process oriented. Distinct from the expert approach, strategy consulting is to a large extent process consulting, focused on guiding the client towards generating and executing its self-developed strategy. However, there also is a more content-related role for the strategy consultant: that of the critical inspirator. Clients are also interested in hearing the consultant's views. But unlike in expert-consulting, the point is not that the consultant should come up with the answers. The point is that he or she can offer an outsider's view that challenges the client's views and that may provide them new insights that they could not have generated by themselves.

This role implies making two types of contributions. The first is to be a source of inspiration. With their specific background and experience, strategy consultants can bring in refreshing opinions and ideas that people within the organization have not thought of. It is this contribution that was emphasized above as part of the traditional approach where it was argued that brainstorming is the *sine qua non* of consulting at McKinsey (Rasiel, 1999, p. 93). Whether it is in brainstorming or elsewhere, part of a strategy consultant's role is to inspire the client with their ideas.

A second contribution is that the strategy consultant also needs to challenge the ideas and views held by the client. People have numerous preconceptions and assumptions, especially if they have worked for a long time in the same industry or organization. This makes them take things for granted that may not be valid. To discover those, the strategy consultant may need to ask repeatedly seemingly naive questions such as 'Why?', 'Why not?' and 'Is that really so?' They may also take the role of devil's advocate who asks people to defend and clarify their positions.

6.5 Communication Channel

A strategy consultant serves as communication channel. People talk to them and they talk to people in the organization, turning the consultant into a *de facto* communication channel between them. And since strategy consultants talk to people at various levels in the organization, they often serve as a channel between people that might otherwise never or rarely talk to each other. This provides them with a unique position that they can use for the benefit of the organization.

Some things are to be avoided because they hurt the process. The first is engaging in gossiping. It doesn't add anything and it can seriously hurt the consultant's reputation as a trusted and dependable outsider – at the client and beyond. Perhaps trivial to mention, but the consultant also shouldn't break trust. This means that, when someone tells them something which is private, that should be kept private, no matter what. And finally, consultants need to make sure that they are not misused as a messenger to someone's personal benefit. A consultant cannot be someone's spokesperson – not the CEO's nor anyone else's – because that undermines their role as a neutral and independent outsider.

What the strategy consultant can do though is to serve as a communication platform for people to make a point that they could otherwise not make. Unlike many employees, the strategy consultant is in direct and regular contact with the top of the organization. This means that they can make sure that a message that is important gets heard by the top. Sometimes the problem is not that people are not in direct contact with the top, but that they don't dare to speak out because it may hurt their position. In that case, the strategy consultant can serve as an anonymous platform where they inform the top without saying from whom they received the message. Or, they may make the message part of their advice or an overall observation without even mentioning that it came from someone specific in the organization.

6.6 Progress Manager

Since strategy consultants are assumed to be experts on strategy generation, the client most likely gives the consultant responsibility over the strategy generation process. This means that a sixth role of a strategy consultant is to make sure that sufficient progress is made and that the steps outlined in Section 5.2 proceed according to plan. Since unexpected events may always happen and since it is hard to know upfront how the strategy generation process will unfold exactly, this also includes adjusting the process when necessary.

Next to taking care of the strategy generation progress, the strategy consultant can also fulfil a role as progress manager in the execution of strategy. Oftentimes, the client takes over responsibility in the execution phase. This makes sense, because it is their strategy and they are indeed the ones who need to execute it. But it may be too early to completely withdraw as a consultant already. In several of my consulting assignments I have experienced that, once you are not involved anymore, the execution process and the attention it receives gradually fade away. The risk is that the strategy will not or will only be partially executed. This makes that its full potential is not achieved and thereby that part of the money and energy spent on strategy generation can be considered wasted.

To avoid this, an effective role of the strategy consultant during strategy execution is that of mentor of the manager or team who take responsibility for the execution of the strategy. In that role, the actual responsibility lies at the client, while the strategy consultant monitors whether progress is as it should be and whether the right things are given priority. Also, the strategy consultant can consult and coach the team how to lead the execution process and step in when help is needed.

6.7 Stable Anchor

The fact that a strategy consultant is involved, virtually always means for an organization that change will come. As implied by its definition, the aim of strategy consulting is providing organizations with support to make changes to achieve unique and sustainable value creation. Without change as result, their added value is limited. This means that there always will be a certain degree of uncertainty and unrest when a strategy consultant is involved. Partly this is useful. As the classical change management approaches tell us, the organization needs some 'unfreezing' and a 'sense of urgency' to prepare it for making changes (Kotter, 1995; Lewin, 1947).

At the same time and exactly for that reason, an additional role for the strategy consultant is to be a stable anchor that the client can rely on. If there is anything the client needs in times of change it is an emotionally stable 'tower of strength' who maintains and creates the necessary calm in the organization. This implies working with confidence and not stressing out. And it also implies approaching everything with a bit of humour and lightness, thereby not taking things too seriously. Even though things may feel extremely important, difficult, uncertain and unique to the client, putting these things in perspective shows they are not. They are rarely life-threatening and hundreds if not thousands of other organizations are going through similar processes at the same time. Adding such dose of groundedness and realism can be exactly what clients need at some times during the process.

6.8 Moral Guide

While it may be a bit controversial, I believe there is also a role for strategy consultants to serve as moral guide. Consultants have their own ethical standards and applying those is what everyone would expect. But I also consider it a strategy consultant's duty to offer clients moral guidance in cases where this seems necessary. The reason is that, if strategy consulting wants to get closer to being a profession, then influencing the client towards more ethical behaviour is part of the job. Therefore, an eighth role of strategy consultants is to be a moral guide and influence the client's ethics. I say 'influence' here, because the consultant cannot take actual responsibility for the client's behaviour.

Being a moral guide doesn't mean preaching or lecturing the client about what is appropriate and what not. That is just as ineffective as trying to provide them with a strategy as an outsider. And since the strategy consultant is usually not hired for moral guidance, preaching and lecturing can quickly lead to dissolving the engagement. Serving as a moral guide, therefore, needs to be subtler and an intrinsic part of strategy consulting.

This starts with the definition of strategy. With its focus on sustainable value creation, this definition provides implicit moral guidance. It makes the organization focus on creating value and on doing this in a sustainable way. Furthermore, since strategy involves the normative 'what should be' question and forming judgements about what is desirable and not, bringing in a normative framework naturally fits strategy consulting. In setting goals or assessing strategy one can bring in, for example, the triple bottom-line (people, profit, planet) (Elkington, 1998), stakeholder theory (Freeman, 1984) or the seventeen sustainable development goals of the United Nations. Using such frameworks helps directing the organization towards more ethical strategy in a natural, implicit way.

6.9 Practical Educator

A final role of strategy consultants is that of practical educator. This role can also be a bit controversial because it implies sharing knowledge and skills with the client in order to improve their strategic capability. Some may consider this undesirable as it makes clients less dependent on the consultant and thereby limit long-term consulting possibilities at the client. But that is exactly why it is desirable and an important last role. As discussed in Section 4.3.4, the long-term outcome of strategy consulting is an improved strategic capability of the client. Taking a role as an educator helps achieving this.

In a time where, due to fast changes and uncertainties, an organization's possibilities for creating and sustaining a competitive advantage are limited, its strategic capability may be one of the only sources to rely on. With such capability, organizations will be able to effectively and efficiently generate and execute strategy in response to the internal and external challenges they face. Looking at the status quo of many organizations, though, such capability is generally underdeveloped – which is one of the reasons strategy consulting has been able to flourish. Strategy consulting can help organizations fill this void.

Being a practical educator doesn't imply being a teacher or lecturer. It implies creating a learning environment and process through which people at the client's organization are stimulated and supported to learn by doing. The co-creative process outlined earlier facilitates such learning because it implies that the strategy consultant collaborates with the client and creates strategy together with them. The first time they go through the process, the strategy consultant will most likely be in the lead. But the more experienced the people at the client become, the better they become at executing the process by themselves.

6.10 Roles Not to Take'

The above nine roles show what it takes to serve as a strategy consultant. At the same time, they also give an idea about the roles the strategy consultant should not have. Nevertheless, for clarity, it is worthwhile mentioning these briefly as well. They are:

- **Decision-maker:** a consultant's role is supportive. They lead the client to finding answers and making decisions, but it is the client's responsibility to make decisions.
- **Scapegoat:** closely related to the first, but nevertheless distinct. With the exceptions of their own mistakes and decisions, consultants are not there to take the blame.
- **Executor:** consultants are there to help, not to execute the work. Of course, they can do some of the required work but their role is to consult, not to provide capacity.
- **Persuader:** it is not the consultant's job to present the client a strategy and convince them that it is the right one. Their job is to help the client generate and execute strategy.
- **Know-it-all:** no one can know everything, even a strategy consultant. Saying 'I don't know' or changing minds when needed will improve their credibility.
- **Show-off:** there is no point in impressing the client with knowledge, jargon or credentials. It is the consultant's behaviour in the nine roles above that will impress them.
- **Rationalist:** explaining reasons and providing evidence for viewpoints is important, but gutfeel is too. Consultants shouldn't ignore it or substitute it with numbers and 'facts'.

- **Neutralist:** consultants want to remain objective. But their opinions count too. They are facilitators, but also part of the process as complete and subjective persons.
- **Joker:** even though humour is important, it is not the consultant's role to be the funniest person in the room. Trying to be this can undermine credibility in any of the nine roles.
- **Colleague:** especially when working together for a long time, consultants may be seen as a part of the organization. But they are not and need to keep their role as outsider.
- **Boss:** consultants are there to serve the client, not the other way around. Therefore, they should avoid being arrogant and snobbish or trying force things upon the client.
- **Acquirer:** it is not the consultant's job to safeguard their position or find the next project. It is to serve the client to the best of their capacity in their current engagement.
- **Echo chamber:** while it may be tempting to agree with everything people say and confirm that, consultants can disagree too. Their different viewpoints are important.
- **Saint:** Even though their moral standards should be high, consultants can also take commercial benefit of situations as long as it keeps their client satisfied.
- **Problem owner:** the more engaged the consultants are, the more they may feel responsible for the client's organization and worry for them. But, at the end, it is their problem.
- **Actor:** consultants shouldn't play being a strategy consultant. They should be a strategy consultant in a way that authentically fits their background, experience, style and personality.

7 Conclusion and Outlook

This Element started with quoting Henry Mintzberg when he said: 'Any chief executive who hires a consultant to give them strategy should be fired.' That might seem a remarkable way to start a book on strategy consulting. But as I hope to have shown in the course of the previous sections, this quote does capture why the traditional approach to strategy consulting isn't so much appreciated and why an alternative approach is needed. It also captures what this alternative approach to strategy consulting is not about: giving organizations a strategy. In this final section, I will briefly conclude what strategy consulting is about instead and where we might want to go from here.

7.1 Whole-Brain, Whole-Person Strategy Consulting

In Section 1 it was argued that the approach to strategy consulting outlined in this Element is a whole-brain, whole-person approach. Throughout the previous sections it has become clearer what is meant with that. Subsequently it was discussed how this starting point affects the purpose of strategy consulting (Section 4), the process of strategy consulting (Section 5) and the roles the strategy consultant plays (Section 6).

The image that we get of strategy consulting from this differs substantially from the traditional approach to strategy consulting that we know from the large consulting firms and the textbooks. It is less fact-based, rational, linear and analytical (left-brain) and more intuitive, creative and holistic (right-brain). And it is not only a cognitive, brain-only activity but just as much a social activity in which personal interactions, empathy and emotions play a central role – making it a whole-person activity.

Compared to existing approaches, this approach comes closest to Maister, Green and Galford's (2000) description of the 'trusted advisor' and Block's (2000) approach to consulting. Both emphasize the importance of right-brain, emotional and social aspects of consulting. The strategy consultant outlined in this Element is a trusted advisor, a person to rely on and with the genuine intent to help the client. But it is a specific type of trusted advisor, focusing on helping the client generate and execute strategy. He or she is an expert in strategy, helping the client's organization achieve unique and sustainable value creation. At the other end of the spectrum, the strategy consultant depicted here is close to being the opposite of the one described by Rasiel and Friga in 'The McKinsey Way' (Rasiel, 1999) and 'The McKinsey Mind' (Rasiel & Friga, 2001). The strategy consultant described in this Element is more empathic, more modest, more cooperative and more serving, and less focused on convincing the client to implement an analytically derived advice.

Much more so than the traditional approach, the approach to strategy consulting in this Element aims for and is based on creating a symbiotic relationship between consultant and client from which both benefit. This relationship is not based on creating dependencies or on a hierarchical idea of one party (the consultant) telling the other party (the client) what to do. Instead, it is a relationship in which equals work together to improve the organization, help each other in doing so and learn from that at the same time (Schein, 2002).

This approach addresses many of the criticisms leveraged against strategy consulting and management consulting at large. As summarized in Section 3.3, there are no less than seventeen of such criticisms: arrogance, pretence of knowledge, pretence of science, lack of integrative view, pretence of creativity, negative orientation, project instead of process-based, slow and linear, disengaged, de-humanized, lacking diversity, no liability and risk, profit-oriented, self-centred, creating dependence, selling fads and unethical. As explained throughout Sections 4, 5 and 6, a whole-brain, whole-person approach directly addresses the large majority of these criticisms.

From the seventeen criticisms, only #11 (lacking diversity) and #12 (no liability and risk) aren't explicitly addressed by the outlined approach. Like the traditional approach, the approach outlined in this Element does not accept liability for the support given and is therefore still relatively free of risk. It was even explicitly argued that decisions are to be made by the client and not by the consultant. Nevertheless, the approach is less susceptible to this criticism than the traditional approach. Through its engaged way of working and focus on sustainable value creation, the approach implies a committed strategy consultant who feels responsible for helping the client. Even though they cannot be held legally accountable for what they do, this sense of responsibility provides an effective substitute that makes criticism #12 less relevant and applicable.

The approach doesn't explicitly address the criticism of lacking diversity either. The approach outlined here is universal. It is agnostic to gender, race or any other characteristic differentiating one person from the other. But exactly this makes that it addresses this criticism indirectly. By its focus on whole-brain consulting, the approach is less masculine than the traditional approach. And by its focus on authentic, whole-person consulting, it embraces everything that makes us a human being. Such appreciative attitude makes the approach more open and tolerant to differences than the traditional approach.

7.2 Caveats and Limitations

In presenting an idealist approach to strategy consulting and contrasting it with the 'traditional approach', I have used a strawman approach. What was described in Section 3 is not the approach as it is used in practice, but the one that is described in the literature. And in just part of the literature. With its origin in 1981, we could argue that Block's (2000) approach to consulting – which differs substantially from the McKinsey type of consulting I refer to as traditional consulting – is traditional too. By leaving it out of the description and focusing on McKinsey's and other large consultancies' approach, I have created a rather outspoken picture of the traditional approach. In practice, strategy consulting will mostly not exactly take place according to this description. However, since it is this approach that we find described in the literature and since it is this approach that is so heavily criticized, I found it useful to summarize it in an outspoken way.

Some may find the alternative approach to strategy consulting outlined in this Element naive or soft. They may object that the world of strategy consulting is a tough world where facts, power, superior intelligence and analysis are needed to tell organizations what is wrong with them and instruct them what to do. The friendlier, personal, participative approach described here, so they might argue, cannot work there. My experience is different though. The approach outlined in this Element is the approach I use in all my consulting work. And the fact that clients stay and return also suggests that it works.

As indicated repeatedly, it is an idealist approach. This means that it doesn't describe strategy consulting as it currently is practiced, but how it could or even should be practiced. But it is certainly not naive or soft. One could argue that the traditional approach is more naive in its limited reliance on cognitive-analytical work and its assumption of superior expertise at the side of the consultant. Embracing that strategy consulting involves our whole brain and whole person is substantially less naive. And regarding softness, the approach is indeed soft on the people side and in terms of style. It relies on friendly relationships with the aim of helping people at the client's organization develop and move forward. But it is tough on the content side. Helping people discover their own limitations and mistakes can be more confronting than simply telling them so. Furthermore, with its long-term emphasis on developing strategic capability, this approach reaches deeper than merely giving strategic advice. It directly intervenes in the way the organization generates and executes strategy. This is everything but soft.

A substantial limitation is the lack of evidence of the effectiveness of the approach. So far, there are not more than anecdotal examples with mostly medium-sized organizations in a handful of industries. Even though the approach is grounded in existing approaches and based on current understanding of how people and organizations work, there is no hard quantitative evidence that it works. But there can't be. Exactly because it is a whole-brain, whole-person approach, it very much depends on the person using the approach whether or not it will work. Not everyone can fulfil all roles of Section 6 and not everyone will be equally equipped to help an organization through all nine steps of the process in Section 5.

Furthermore, because strategy consulting is a relational activity between client and consultant, it will also depend on the specific relation between them whether this approach works. What works for one client–consultant relationship, may not work for another. Equally important to realize is that both sides respond to each other. If the strategy consultant adopts the traditional approach, the client will respond in a way that fits that approach. And if the strategy consultant adopts the approach of this Element, the client will respond differently.

This means that the choice for the traditional approach or the approach outlined here is largely a choice of paradigm – how one chooses to look at the world and approach it accordingly. Some might feel more comfortable using the traditional approach, believe it is the right approach and apply it accordingly. Others might feel more comfortable applying the approach outlined in this Element. This implies the approach will not be for everyone. As it is evident, the traditional approach doesn't work for me. And as it is also evident, I am convinced that the alternative approach outlined here is the better route. But convincing anyone of that is not the main point of this Element. The main point is that it sketches an alternative to the traditional approach that may be viable too. And because this alternative approach is a direct response to the various criticisms leveraged against the traditional approach, it is less sensitive to these criticisms and can therefore be seen as a move forward.

7.3 Moving Forward

This Element has described an approach to strategy consulting that deviates from the mainstream approach with the intention of sketching an alternative that addresses its main limitations. The fact that it is still an idealist approach, rather than a description of the status quo, means there is substantial work to do should we want to move forward in the described direction. In this final section, I will present five possible routes that, together, can help strategy consulting become a more relevant and appreciated profession.

7.3.1 Towards a Profession

Section 1 asked whether strategy consulting is currently a profession and whether it should be. The conclusion there was that it currently is not, but that it is something worthwhile striving for. In getting there, we can think of two approaches: a systemic top-down approach and an individual bottom-up approach. Given the vested interests and the complexity and magnitude of the required changes, it was argued that the first approach will not be viable. This means that, if strategy consulting is to get closer to being a profession, the only viable route is the individual, bottom-up route.

When evaluated against the seven traits of a profession that were mentioned in Section 1.3.3, we can observe that the approach outlined in this Element is a step forward. It doesn't lead to professional institutions, standardized training, a shared body of knowledge or a code of ethics. But it does imply greater professional liability, self-regulation and focus on the greater good. Not by establishing rules, but by suggesting an approach in which these characteristics of a profession are built-in. When strategy consulting is approached in a whole-brain, whole-person way, by adopting the purpose (Section 4), process (Section 5) and roles (Section 6) outlined in this Element, it will *de facto* get closer to a profession.

In realizing this, the key focus is on mindset and informal changes. The formalities of a profession – institutions, standardized training, a shared body of knowledge and a code of ethics – are artificial and meaningless if the underling mindset and intention are not in place. On the other hand, if mindset and intention are in place, the need for these formal aspects significantly decreases. But mindset and intentions are not easily changed. This begs the question as to how to move forward to realize the suggested changes. Education is the answer. Not merely formal education, but also self-education, coaching and learning-by -doing. This includes teaching the approach above at business schools; using it in practice in one's own strategy consulting; and communicating about it through books, articles, blogs or any other means so that others can take notice of it and learn.

7.3.2 The Role of Technology

This Element has paid no attention technology. I have refrained from that because the approach itself does not depend on technology. At the same time, though, there are various technological developments – especially in IT – that can help advance the approach and its effectiveness. Examples are big data and analytics, artificial and assisted intelligence, virtual and augmented reality, digitalization and virtualization, block chain and cybersecurity. Most large consulting firms are in the process of adopting these technologies in their consulting practices, especially the first. Data are getting increasing attention and a lot of trust is put in the possibilities of data-driven consulting. I am sceptical. Not about the fact that we can obtain and effectively process much more detailed data about organizations, but about the importance of such data for consulting. In the light of the approach outlined in this Element, data are merely a small fraction of what is needed. Instead, strategy consulting is much more a social process, triggering people's creativity and intuition in conceiving and realizing what is, what could be, what should be and what will be.

Armbrüster and Kipping (2002) and Van den Bosch, Baaij, and Volberda (2005) are pessimistic about the impact of IT on strategy consulting. As they observe, the established strategy consulting firms are under pressure because their knowledge accumulation-based expert approach is quickly losing relevance. As a result, as far as it concerns pure strategy consulting, there only seems to be place for smaller niche players, they argue. To some extent, I share this pessimism because the arguments given about traditional large consulting firms are convincing. However, I am optimistic about the commercial chances for strategy consulting in general.

With the approach outlined in this Element, there is no real advantage in being a large firm. Standardization of methods, knowledge accumulation and knowledge efficiencies are not relevant when using it. Furthermore, working with consultants that are largely interchangeable – as is one of the principles in large consultancies – is even a disadvantage. The ability to establish personal relationships as a trusted strategy consultant that guides clients in generating and executing strategy is gaining relevance. And that might be realized in smaller firms and independents focusing on particular niches. Given the tremendous possibility for improving organizations' strategic capability, there is an enormous market potential for such type of strategy consulting.

There is one alternative way in which IT can have a profound effect on strategy consulting. The approach outlined earlier can be adopted without any significant technology. The traditional brown papers and post-its techniques can work effectively. However, the approach can be more effective once a 'digital twin' of the organization exist at the strategic level. Once organizations have their strategy represented in a living, digital version, the iterative participative approach can work more effectively. In the same way as other software systems such as ERP, financial or CRM systems, for example, create a virtual representation of an organization's resources, finances and customers that can be managed, this digital strategy twin can help to manage strategy in a truly dynamic way. Making the implementation and use of such digital strategy twin part of strategy consulting, can help make it a significant leap forward.

7.3.3 Advancing the Approach

The fact that the approach outlined in this Element directly addresses most of the seventeen critiques leveraged against the traditional approach makes it a step forward. Furthermore, also when we compare it against Greiner, Motamedi and Jamieson's (2011) outline of new consulting roles and practices that are needed in today's world, it can be seen as a step forward. They argue the following thirteen transitions are needed for effective consulting in today's dynamic environment:

1. From consultant as expert to consultant as guide.
2. From long-cycle consulting to fast-cycle consulting.
3. From content or process expert to content and process facilitator.
4. From simple and incremental to complex and discontinuous.
5. From single entities to transorganizations.
6. From hierarchical organizations to network organizations.

7. From command and control to self organizing.
8. From boss as client to organization as client.
9. From labour intensive to information-process intensive.
10. From doctor–patient to resource partners.
11. From study–analyse–recommend to joint data–diagnosis.
12. From survey research to action learning
13. From plan first, then implement to plan and implement together.

When we compare the approach outlined in this Element to these thirteen transitions, it can be concluded that it follows the large majority of them. The approach indeed makes the transition from the consultant as expert to the consultant as guide, from long-cycle consulting to fast-cycle consulting etc. Thus, also in the light of these recommended transitions, the approach is a significant step forward compared to the traditional consulting approach.

But it also requires further advancement and strengthening. To date it is based on literature, previous research and personal experiences of a handful of consultants. This means that the creative and intellectual power of the masses has been barely tapped. Along those lines, this Element is an open invitation to others – scholars, consultants, leaders and anyone else – for adding, amending or critiquing the approach with the intent to further advancing it.

Next to this general call for advancing the approach, there is one aspect that requires specific attention. Two of Greiner, Motamedi and Jamieson's (2011) suggested transitions have not been addressed yet: from single entities to transorganizations (#5) and from hierarchical to network organizations (#6). These two transitions are related. Both signal a change from organizations as closed hierarchical systems to organizations as open networks. While the approach outlined in this Element could be compatible with this transition, it doesn't specifically address the challenges of open, networked organizations. Therefore, further advancement is needed to make the approach tailored for situations where multiple organizations, networks or ecosystems are the client instead of a single organization.

7.3.4 Strategy Consulting Research

Given its significant volume and impact, it is remarkable how little research has been conducted on strategy consulting. There are only very few publications specifically about strategy consulting and even fewer of them concern empirical research. There are some historical studies of the development of strategy consulting (Armbrüster & Kipping, 2002; David, 2012), a couple of case studies (Blom & Lundgren, 2013; Seidel, 2000; Van den Bosch et al., 2005) and some older assessments of strategy consultant's impact (Delany, 1995; Leontiades &

Tezel, 1988; Payne & Lumsden, 1987). But that is all. Of course, there is the larger body of research on management consulting, but focused on strategy consulting there is hardly any research published. Along those lines, the general direction that can be given is to actually conduct research specifically on strategy consulting. Whether it is conceptual, qualitative, quantitative or design-oriented research, the mere importance of strategy consulting warrants more of it.

Even though strategy consulting can be approached from various research paradigms and approaches, it seems most natural that this at least occurs as part of the 'strategy as practice' tradition that has emerged over the past three decades (Carter, Clegg, & Kornberger, 2008; Chia & Holt, 2006; Jarzabkowski, 2004; Whittington, 1996). With its focus on the 'praxis, practices and practitioners' of strategy, one would expect a significant volume of studies on strategy consulting there. While sometimes implied or referred to in strategy as practice studies, though, no dedicated work on strategy consulting has been published so far as part of this tradition.

Whether such research has actually not taken place is hard to tell. Because the kind of research that may be required is both challenging to conduct and challenging to get published. Obtaining detailed insights into strategy consulting requires deep involvement and interventionist approaches such as action learning and design-oriented research. Conducting such research requires being a strategy consultant or following them very closely. Being a strategy scholar–practitioner–trainer myself, I have experienced how challenging this is. This is especially the case since, when involved with a client, the consultant's primary emphasis is on helping the client, not on conducting research. Nevertheless, it can be done and this Element is largely a result of my own attempt to do so. It is based on my own action learning taking place by applying the process and roles outlined above, reflecting upon them and adjusting them accordingly. While I would qualify it as research, and certainly as relevant research, I cannot think of any impactful journal that would accept the kind of research done because it lacks the traditional rigor that is expected. Along those lines, the directions that can be given are to (a) conduct more of such interventionist kind of research, (b) do it in more systematic and documented way and (c) help further legitimizing the methods needed for it.

7.3.5 Moving Strategy Forward as a Field

The progress that can be made with advancing the field of strategy consulting depends on the state of the field of strategy at large. As numerous others have argued, the field of strategy is not in a particularly good shape. Criticisms leveraged include that it is fragmented, not relevant enough, too narrow, too much focused on analytical tools and even harmful for practice (Bettis, 1991; Ghoshal & Moran, 1996; Mahoney & McGahan, 2007; Oxley et al., 2010; Powell, 2003; Vaara & Durand, 2012).

Hitherto, strategy is still mostly presented as a cognitive-analytical skill that largely consists of the application of a wide range of different frameworks. One just has to look at some of the major strategy textbooks to see this (Whittington et al., 2017). Given the focus on cognitive-analytical skills and extensive use of frameworks and given the impact of strategy consulting on the contents of strategy textbooks and training, we should not be surprised that strategy consulting has this same bias. Therefore, in order to bring strategy consulting forward, we also need to bring the field of strategy forward. This requires new, more integrative and dynamic approaches to strategy generation and execution. The nine-step approach outlined above is my personal attempt to achieve this (Kraaijenbrink, 2015, 2018). In this same spirit, others should develop better ones and thereby help both strategy and strategy consulting move forward.

References

Abrahamson, E. (1996). Management fashion. *Academy of Management Review, 21*(1), 254–285.

Ackermann, F. & Eden, C. (2011). *Making Strategy: Mapping Out Strategic Success*. London: Sage.

Alvesson, M. (2002). Professionalism and politics in management consultancy work. In T. Clark & R. Fincham (eds.), *Critical Consulting: New Perspectives on the Management Advice Industry* (pp. 228–246). Oxford: Blackwell.

Argyris, C., Putnam, R., & McLain Smith, D. (1985). *Action Science*. San Francisco: Jossey-Bass.

Argyris, C. & Schön, D. A. (1978). *Organizational Learning: A Theory of Action Perspective*. Reading, MA: Addison-Wesley.

Armbrüster, T. & Kipping, M. (2002). Strategy consulting at the crossroads: technical change and shifting market conditions for top-level advice. *International Studies of Management & Organization, 32*(4), 19–42.

Baaij, M. (2013). *An Introduction to Management Consultancy*. London: Sage.

Barney, J. B. (1991). Firm resources and sustained competitive advantage. *Journal of Management, 17*(1), 99–120.

Bettis, R. A. (1991). Strategic management and the straightjacket: an editorial essay. *Organization Science, 2*(3), 315–319.

Birkinshaw, J. & Gibson, C. (2004). Building ambidexterity into an organization. *MIT Sloan Management Review, 45*, 47–55.

Block, P. (2000). *Flawless Consulting: A Guide to Getting Your Expertise Used*. San Francisco, CA: Pfeiffer.

Blom, M. & Lundgren, M. (2013). Strategy consultants doing strategy: how status and visibility affect strategizing. *African Journal of Business Management, 7*(14), 1144–1160.

Brown, T. (2008). Design thinking. *Harvard Business Review, 86*(6), 84.

Carter, C., Clegg, S. R., & Kornberger, M. (2008). So!apbox: editorial essays: strategy as practice? *Strategic Organization, 6*(1), 83–99.

Chia, R. & Holt, R. (2006). Strategy as practical coping: a Heideggerian perspective. *Organization Studies, 27*(5), 635.

Cialdini, R. B. (2006). *Influence: The Psychology of Persuasion*. New York: Harper Business.

Clark, T. (1995). *Managing Consultants: Consultancy as the Management of Impressions*. Buckingham: Open University Press.

Clark, T., Bhatanacharioen, P., & Greatbatch, D. (2012). Management gurus as celebrity consultants. In M. Kipping & T. Clark (eds.), *The Oxford Handbook of Management Consulting* (pp. 347–364). Oxford: Oxford University Press.

Clark, T. & Fincham, R. (eds.). (2002). *Critical Consulting: New Perspectives on the Management Advice Industry*. Oxford: Blackwell Business.

Cooperrider, D. & Srivastva, S. (1987). Appreciative inquiry in organizational life. In R.W. Woodman & W.A. Pasmore (eds.), *Research in Organizational Change and Development, Vol. 1* (pp. 129–169). Greenwich: JAI Press.

David, R. J. (2012). Institutional change and the growth of strategy consulting in the United States. In M. Kipping & T. Clark (eds.), *The Oxford Handbook of Management Consulting* (pp. 71–92). Oxford: Oxford University Press.

Delany, E. (1995). Strategy consultants – Do they add value? *Long Range Planning, 28*(6), 99–106.

DiMaggio, P. J. & Powell, W. W. (1983). The iron cage revisited: institutional isomorphism and collective rationality in organizational fields. *American Sociological Review, 48*(2), 147–160.

Elkington, J. (1998). *Cannibals with Forks: The Triple Bottom Line of 21st Century Business*. Oxford: Capstone Publishing Limited.

Faust, M. (2012). Sociological perspectives on management consulting. In M. Kipping & T. Clark (eds.), *The Oxford Handbook of Management Consulting* (pp. 139–164). Oxford: Oxford University Press.

Follett, M. P. (1924). *Creative Experience*. London: Longmans, Green.

Follett, M. P., Fox, E. M., & Urwick, L. (1973). *Dynamic Administration: The Collected Papers of Mary Parker Follett*. London: Pitman Publishing.

Ford, J. D. & Ford, L. W. (2010). Stop blaming resistance to change and start using it. *Organizational Dynamics, 39*(1), 24–36.

Ford, J. D., Ford, L. W., & D'Amelio, A. (2008). Resistance to change: the rest of the story. *Academy of Management Review, 33*(2), 362–377.

Freeman, R. E. (1984). *Strategic Management: A Stakeholder Approach*. Cambridge, UK: Cambridge University Press.

Ghoshal, S. & Moran, P. (1996). Bad for practice: a critique of the transaction cost theory. *Academy of Management Review, 21*(1), 13–47.

Greiner, L., Motamedi, K., & Jamieson, D. (2011). New consultant roles and processes in a 24/7 world. *Organizational Dynamics, 40*(3), 165.

Hagenmeyer, U. (2007). Integrity in management consulting: a contradiction in terms? *Business Ethics: A European Review, 16*(2), 107–113.

Hambrick, D. C. & Fredrickson, J. W. (2001). Are you sure you have a strategy? *The Academy of Management Executive, 15*(4), 48–59.

Jarzabkowski, P. (2004). Strategy as practice: recursiveness, adaptation, and practices-in-use. *Organization Studies, 25*(4), 529.

Jung, N. & Kieser, A. (2012). Consultants in the management fashion arena. In M. Kipping & T. Clark (eds.), *The Oxford Handbook of Management Consulting* (pp. 327–346). Oxford: Oxford University Press.

Khurana, R. (2007). *From Higher Aims to Hired Hands: The Social Transformation of American Business Schools and the Unfulfilled Promise of Management as a Profession*. Princeton: Princeton University Press.

Kim, W. C. & Mauborgne, R. (2005). *Blue Ocean Strategy: How to Create Uncontested Market Space and Make the Competition Irrelevant*. Boston, US: Harvard Business School Press.

Kipping, M. & Clark, T. (2012). *The Oxford Handbook of Management Consulting*: Oxford University Press.

Kirkpatrick, I., Muzio, D., & Ackroyd, S. (2012). Professions and professionalism in management consulting. In M. Kipping & T. Clark (eds.), *The Oxford Handbook of Management Consulting* (pp. 187–206). Oxford: Oxford University Press.

Kotter, J. P. (1995). Leading change: why transformation efforts fail. *Harvard Business Review, 73*(2), 59–67.

Kraaijenbrink, J. (2015). *The Strategy Handbook, Part 1: Strategy Generation*. Doetinchem: Effectual Strategy Press.

Kraaijenbrink, J. (2018). *The Strategy Handbook, Part 2: Strategy Execution*. Doetinchem: Effectual Strategy Press.

Kraaijenbrink, J., Spender, J.-C., & Groen, A. J. (2010). The resource-based view: a review and assessment of its critiques. *Journal of Management, 36* (1), 349–372.

Kubr, M. (2002). *Management Consulting: A Guide to the Profession*. New Delhi: Bookwell Publications.

Lemann, N. (1999). The kids in the conference room: how McKinsey & Company became the next big step. *The New Yorker* (18 & 25 October), 216. https://www.newyorker.com/magazine/1999/10/18/the-kids-in-the-conference-room

Leontiades, M. & Tezel, A. (1988). CEOs perceptions of strategy consultants. *Business Forum, 14*(1), 51–53.

Lewin, K. (1947). Frontiers in group dynamics: concept, method and reality in social science; social equilibria and social change. *Human Relations, 1*(1), 5–41.

Lewin, K. (1948). *Resolving Social Conflicts; Selected Papers on Group Dynamics*. New York: Harper & Row.

Mahoney, J. T. & McGahan, A. M. (2007). The field of strategic management within the evolving science of strategic organization. *Strategic Organization, 5*(1), 79–99.

Maister, D. H., Green, C. H., & Galford, R. M. (2000). *The Trusted Advisor.* New York: Simon and Schuster.

March, J. G. (1991). Exploration and exploitation in organizational learning. *Organization Science, 2*(1), 71–87.

Martin, R. L. (2015). Stop distinguishing between execution and strategy. *Harvard Business Review*(March). https://hbr.org/2015/03/stop-distinguishing-between-execution-and-strategy

Maslow, A. H. (1970). *Motivation and Personality* (2nd ed.). New York: Harper & Row.

McDonald, D. (2013). *The Firm: The Story of McKinsey and its Secret Influence on American Business.* London: Simon and Schuster.

McGrath, R. G. (2013). Transient advantage. *Harvard Business Review, 91*(6), 62–70.

McGregor, D. (1960). *The Human Side of Enterprise.* New York: McGraw-Hill.

McKenna, C. (2012). Strategy followed structure: management consulting and the creation of a market for 'strategy', 1950–2000. In S.J. Kahl, Brian S. Silverman & M.A. Cusumano (eds.), *History and Strategy*, Volume 29 (pp. 153–186): Bingley: Emerald Group Publishing Limited.

McKenna, C. D. (2006). *The World's Newest Profession: Management Consulting in the Twentieth Century.* Cambridge: Cambridge University Press.

Micklethwait, J. & Woodridge, A. (1996). *The Witch Doctors: What the Management Gurus are Saying, Why it Matters and How to Make Sense of it.* London: Heinemann.

Micklethwait, J. & Wooldridge, A. (1996). *The Witch Doctors: Making Sense of the Management Gurus.* London: Crown Business.

Minto, B. (2009). *The Pyramid Principle: Logic in Writing and Thinking.* Harlow: Pearson Education.

Mintzberg, H. (1987). Crafting strategy. *Harvard Business Review*(July-August), 66–75. https://hbr.org/1987/07/crafting-strategy

Mintzberg, H. & Waters, J. A. (1985). Of strategies, deliberate and emergent. *Strategic Management Journal, 6*(3), 257–272.

Newton, R. (2010). *The Management Consultant: Mastering the Art of Consultancy.* Harlow: Pearson Education.

Nikolova, N. & Devinney, T. (2012). The nature of client-consultant interaction: a critical review. In M. Kipping & T. Clark (eds.), *The Oxford Handbook of Management Consulting* (pp. 389–410). Oxford: Oxford University Press.

O'Mahoney, J. & Markham, C. (2013). *Management Consultancy.* Oxford, UK: Oxford University Press.

O'Reilly III, C. A. & Tushman, M. L. (2004). The ambidextrous organization. *Harvard Business Review*, April, 74–81. https://hbr.org/2004/04/the-ambi dextrous-organization

O'Shea, J. E. & Madigan, C. (1998). *Dangerous Company: Management Consultants and the Businesses They Save and Ruin*. New York: Penguin Putnam.

Osterwalder, A. & Pigneur, Y. (2010). *Business Model Generation: A Handbook for Visionaries, Game Changers, and Challengers*: Hoboken: John Wiley & Sons.

Oxley, J. E., Rivkin, J. W., Ryall, M. D., & Strategy Research Initiative. (2010). The strategy research initiative: recognizing and encouraging high-quality research in strategy. *Strategic Organization*, 8(4), 377–386.

Payne, A. & Lumsden, C. (1987). Strategy consulting – A shooting star? *Long Range Planning*, 20(3), 53–64.

Peters, T. J., Waterman, R. H., & Jones, I. (1982). *In Search of Excellence: Lessons from America's Best-run Companies*. New York: Harper and Row.

Pinault, L. (2009). *Consulting Demons: Inside the Unscrupulous World of Global Corporate Consulting*. New York: Harper Collins.

Porter, M. E. (1980). *Competitive Strategy: Techniques for Analyzing Industries and Competitors*. New York: The Free Press.

Porter, M. E. (1991). Towards a dynamic theory of strategy. *Strategic Management Journal*, 12(Special Issue, Winter), 95–117.

Powell, T. C. (2003). Strategy without ontology. *Strategic Management Journal*, 24(3), 285–291.

Prahalad, C. K. & Hamel, G. (1990). The core competence of the corporation. *Harvard Business Review*, 68(3), 79–91.

Raisch, S. & Birkinshaw, J. (2008). Organizational ambidexterity: antecedents, outcomes, and moderators. *Journal of Management*, 34(3), 375–409.

Rasiel, E. M. (1999). *The McKinsey Way: Using the Techniques of the World's Top Strategic Consultants to Help You and Your Business*. New York: McGraw-Hill.

Rasiel, E. M. & Friga, P. N. (2001). *The McKinsey Mind*. New York, NY: McGraw-Hill.

Rousseau, D. M. (2012). Designing a better business school: channelling Herbert Simon, addressing the critics, and developing actionable knowledge for professionalizing managers. *Journal of Management Studies*, 49(3), 600–618.

Rumelt, R. (2011). *Good Strategy/Bad Strategy: The Difference and Why it Matters*. New York: Profile Books.

Saam, N. J. (2012). Economics approaches to management consulting. In M. Kipping & T. Clark (eds.), *The Oxford Handbook of Management Consulting* (pp. 207–224). Oxford: Oxford University Press.

Schein, E. H. (2002). Consulting: what should it mean? In T. Clark & R. Fincham (eds.), *Critical Consulting: New Perspectives on the Management Advice Industry* (pp. 21–27). Oxford: Blackwell Business.

Schoemaker, P. J. (1995). Scenario planning: a tool for strategic thinking. *Sloan Management Review, 36*, 25–40.

Seidel, V. (2000). Moving from design to strategy: the four roles of design-led strategy consulting. *Design Management Journal, 11*(2), 35–40.

Sinek, S. (2009). *Start with Why: How Great Leaders Inspire Everyone to Take Action*. New York: Penguin.

Spender, J.-C. (2007). Management as a regulated profession: an essay. *Journal of Management Inquiry, 16*(1), 32–42.

Spender, J.-C. (2014). *Business Strategy: Managing Uncertainty, Opportunity, and Enterprise*. Oxford: Oxford University Press.

Steele, F. (1975). *Consulting for Organizational Change*. Amherst, MA: University of Massachusetts Press.

Taylor, F. W. (1911). *The Principles of Scientific Management*, New York: Harper & Brothers.

Teece, D. J., Pisano, G. P., & Shuen, A. (1997). Dynamic capabilities and strategic management. *Strategic Management Journal, 18*(7), 509–533.

Vaara, E. & Durand, R. (2012). How to connect strategy research with broader issues that matter? *Strategic Organization, 10*(3), 248–255.

Van den Bosch, F. A., Baaij, M. G., & Volberda, H. W. (2005). How knowledge accumulation has changed strategy consulting: strategic options for established strategy consulting firms. *Strategic Change, 14*(1), 25–34.

Waterman, R. H. (1982). The seven elements of strategic fit. *Journal of Business Strategy, 2*(3), 69–73.

Waterman, R. H., Peters, T. J., & Phillips, J. R. (1980). Structure is not organization. *Business Horizons, 23*(3), 14–26.

Weiden, E. F. (2014). *Folienkrieg und Bullshitbingo: Handbuch für Unternehmensberater, Opfer und Angehörige*. München: Piper Verlag.

Weiss, A. (1992). *Million Dollar Consulting: The Professional's Guide to Growing a Practice*. New York: McGraw-Hill.

Whitney, D. & Cooperrider, D. (2005). *Appreciative Inquiry: A Positive Revolution in Change*. Oakland CA: Berrett-Koehler Publishers.

Whittington, R. (1996). Strategy as practice. *Long Range Planning, 29*(5), 731–735.

Whittington, R., Johnson, G., Scholes, K., Angwin, D., & Regnér, P. (2017). *Exploring Strategy*. Harlow: Pearson.

Wickham, P. A. & Wilcock, J. (2016). *Management Consulting: Delivering an Effective Project*. Harlow, UK: Pearson Education Limited.

Cambridge Elements ☰

Business Strategy

J.-C. Spender
Kozminski University

J.-C. Spender is a visiting scholar at Kozminski University and a research Professor, Kozminski University. He has been active in the business strategy field since 1971 and is the author or co-author of seven books and numerous papers. His principal academic interest is in knowledge-based theories of the private sector firm, and managing them.

About the series

Business strategy's reach is vast, and important too since wherever there is business activity there is strategizing. As a field, strategy has a long history from medieval and colonial times to today's developed and developing economies. This series offers a place for interesting and illuminating research including industry and corporate studies, strategizing in service industries, the arts, the public sector and the new forms of Internet-based commerce. It also covers today's expanding gamut of analytic techniques.

Cambridge Elements ≡

Business Strategy

Elements in the series

A full series listing is available at: www.cambridge.org/EBUS

Printed in the United States
By Bookmasters